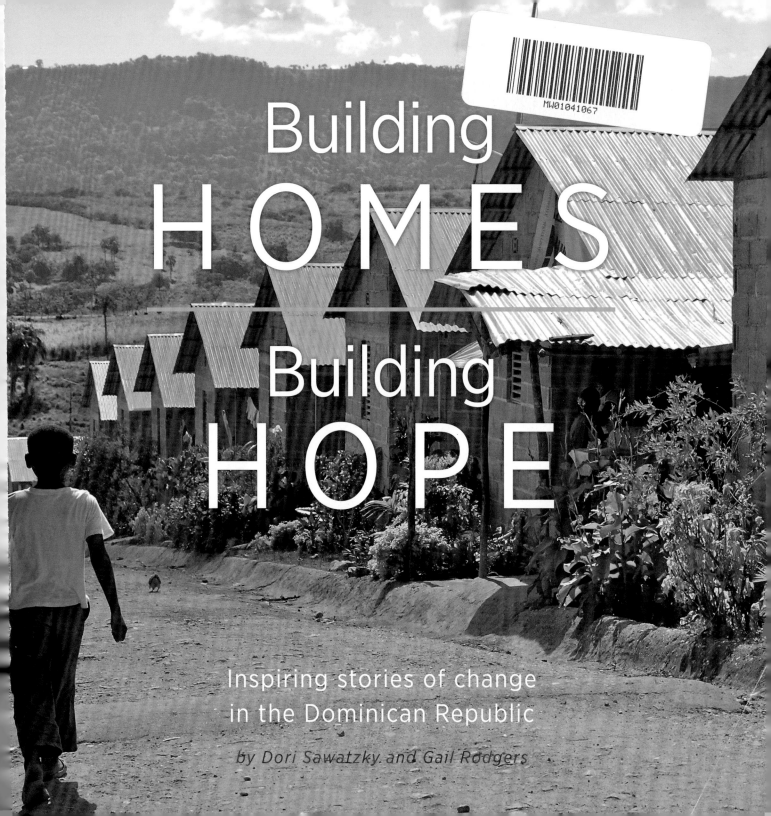

Building
HOMES

Building
HOPE

Inspiring stories of change
in the Dominican Republic

by Dori Sawatzky and Gail Rodgers

Photos generously provided by
Lorel Giesbrecht
Christa Giesbrecht
Onofrio Miccolis

ISBN
978-1-4602-2052-8 (Paperback)
978-1-4602-2053-5 (eBook)

Produced by:

FriesenPress

Suite 300 – 852 Fort Street
Victoria, BC, Canada V8W 1H8

www.friesenpress.com

Distributed to the trade by The Ingram Book Company

Dedicated to YOU, the reader
and
to the many unnamed participants in this exceptional story

All proceeds from the sale of this book will go towards
the work of the Samaritan Foundation

Contents

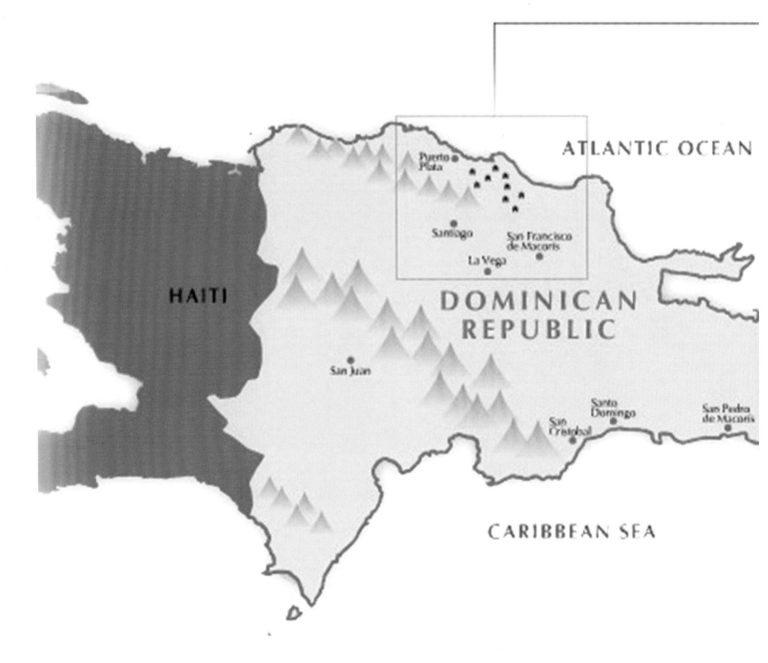

ATLANTIC OCEAN

HAITI

DOMINICAN
REPUBLIC

Puerto
Plata

Santiago

San Francisco
de Macorís

La Vega

San Juan

Santo
Domingo

San Pedro
de Macorís

San
Cristóbal

CARIBBEAN SEA

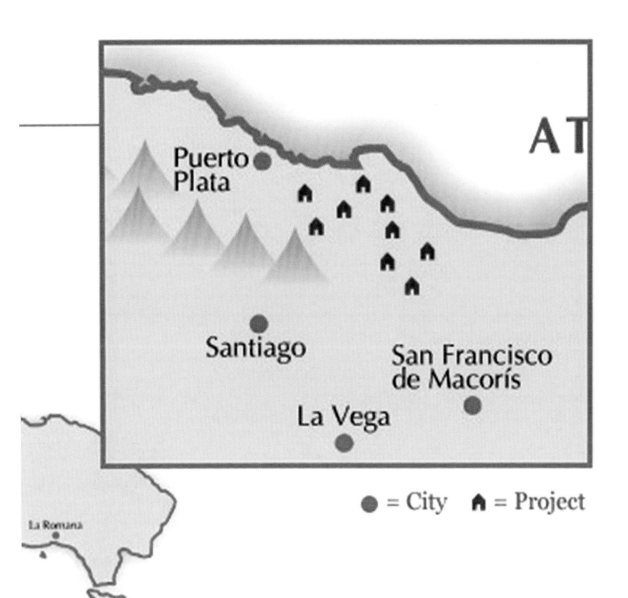

Puerto Plata

A T

Santiago

San Francisco
de Macorís

La Vega

La Romana

● = City 🏠 = Project

A NOTE FROM DORI

Heart wrenching poverty has been a part of the human story since time immemorial. Children's faces devoid of hope or happiness flash across our screens. Both around the globe and across the street, there are millions whose only thought and goal is to eke out a daily existence, to keep their family alive for one more day. Stories abound of caring individuals and humanitarian agencies that are able to address some of the need, that bring relief to those they can reach, and we are thankful for each one. What makes this story of reaching out any different from the many others being told?

This is our story. This is our ring-side seat to some amazing events that are happening in the Dominican Republic. We are witnessing what happens when ordinary people care enough to really see the needs of an impoverished and suffering people, and are motivated to help. Because they care, they are giving of their time, their talents or their resources to bring positive, sustainable change to this little corner of the world.

In this age of instant technology, it takes a concerted effort to remain unaware and untouched by the affliction and agony that poverty inflicts upon its hapless victims.

According to 2012 statistics from the United Nations, 50% of the world's population lives on less than $2.50 per day and 80% lives on less than $10.00 per day. Over one billion people have inadequate access to water, and each day 22,000 children die because of poverty's heartless appetite. This is humankind's greatest challenge.[1]

Population. Percentages. Humankind. They are all such distancing words. They allow us to read the numbers and avoid seeing the people. They allow us to skim over the fact that they are mothers, fathers, children, and grandparents. Though they are people just like us, they are forced to greet each morning with desperate questions. "Will I find food today?" "Will my baby live through this day?" "Where will I find water?"

Statistics for the Dominican Republic do not paint a picture as dire perhaps as some other poverty-stricken countries. Here the presence of a performing democratic government provides access to established offices and officials who are able to facilitate development, though not without a good measure of perseverance.

The challenges in the Dominican Republic are great. Forty-two percent of the population lives below the poverty line, with an average income of approximately $2 to $4 per day. In seeking to address the problem, the Dominican government has initiated an anti-poverty program, and yet less than 3% of GDP (gross domestic product) has been spent on education, and less than 1% on healthcare.[2]

Human trafficking for the purposes of sexual exploitation and forced labour is a growing problem in the Dominican Republic. It has become a destination for sexual predators that puts men, women, and children at risk. Severe discrimination against Haitian migrants and their descendants contributes to the violence and unrest in their society and broadens the gap between the rich and the poor. Because of inaccessibility to clean water and health care, rural Dominicans suffer high rates of diarrhea, respiratory illness, and hypertension. Much work and education is needed to stop the rampant spread of tuberculosis, HIV/AIDS, and other sexually transmitted diseases.

But this is not a bad news story! This is a good news story! A story of inspiration! Through the work of the Samaritan Foundation[3] and many other organizations and individuals, the visible face of change is evident in the Dominican Republic. People from all walks of life are uniting in the common purpose of bringing hope and a hand up to those caught in the clutches of extreme poverty.

My husband, Ben Sawatzky, and I were invited to step into this incredible story that was already in motion. We in turn invited others, one of whom is my dear friend and co-author, Gail Rodgers.

This is a collection of stories of people who were touched by the needs they saw around them, and then listened to the whispering of God as He nudged them to be His hands and feet on earth. Every time someone reaches out to bring love and hope to another human being, another story is written. It is our hope that these vignettes might touch your heart to look afresh at your world, to be encouraged and inspired by the stories your life is writing, and those yet waiting to be written.

We invite you to join us in this inspiring journey.

Dori Sawatzky

Part One

AN UNEXPECTED INTERRUPTION

"A wrong turn that turned out to be very right."

-Elio Madonia

Maria wiped the sweat from her face. The hot afternoon sun, the crying baby, and two days without food made her feel faint. She must get these jugs of water up the hill. Though the water was brown and murky it was the only water she had to give her children. It was the only water she could cook with, if she could find rice to cook. Deep weariness ached within her. As she pulled the last jug inside the makeshift door of her tiny shanty, the rain began to pelt down. Too often she had witnessed the cruelty of the fast-rising river rushing in to snatch homes and lives into its ruthless embrace. Would she have to run from the swelling river again tonight? Hard days stretched into long weary years as Maria simply put one foot in front of the other. Her only hope was her faith that God would hear the cry for help that arose daily from her desperate heart.

In the early 1980s, in the dismal settlement of Charamicos, near Sosua, Dominican Republic, the people lived in deplorable conditions. Their makeshift mud and twig shelters lacked even the basic necessities of life. There was no electricity and no access to clean water. Raw sewage, mingled with frequent rains, washed down the narrow pathways between their hovels. In spite of the apparent hopelessness of their situation, the faithful few would gather together daily to plead with God to help them, knowing that He was their only hope in this dismal place that they

4

called home. So they prayed. Pastor Reyes Peña shared in the desperation of his small congregation. He was as hungry, poor, and weary as they were. On this day he squared his shoulders and stepped out to join the dedicated assembly that gathered in the church. Today would be no different than any other day, he thought. Yet it was different.

This day, during prayer, one of the men was given a vision, an image in his mind that carried with it a sense of promise, of hope for their future. "A white man from a distant land with a lot of snow will come to help us. God will send him." From that day on, with faith, they began to pray for that man to come.

The story continued, but in a setting thousands of miles to the north.

Elio Madonia was a prosperous businessman from Ontario, who worked in church ministry both in Canada and other parts of the world. His wife, Lena, was very ill most of their married life and devoted the strength that she was given to raising their eight children. As their retirement years began to creep up on them, Elio had a growing desire to take more time to care for his wife, the love of his life. He also felt a greater longing to give back to God in gratitude for the many blessings he had received.

In 1988 Elio retired, and to celebrate, he and Lena traveled to the warm Caribbean island of the Dominican Republic. The resort they chose to visit was near the city of Sosua, in the province of Puerto Plata, very near the village of Charamicos.

Here Elio was interrupted by God.

One day he decided to take a stroll out of the resort to enjoy the beauty of the tropical countryside, but somehow he got lost. He stood in the hot Dominican sun with a furrowed brow. He had meant only to take a short walk. How could he have ventured into this slum? How could he have put himself in possible danger? Dark eyes watched him curiously. Gradually his surroundings sank in. Never had he seen or even imagined the existence of such poverty. His heart broke for the people forced to live in the stench and squalor of a lifetime of hardship and deprivation. The shacks. The faces lined with weariness. Eyes dulled by hopelessness. The garbage. The filth. The smell. He watched a father furtively stealing food from a pig trough to feed his family. It gripped his heart as nothing ever had. Slowly he turned to find his way back to the resort. Clean and safe, he would resume his holiday. Yet what he had witnessed would not leave him. His soul was troubled. "Lord," he cried out, "how can You let children You have created live like this?"

The answer that stirred in his heart was clearly the Lord's reply. "What are you going to do about it?"

Elio could have put on his swimsuit and swum hard in the warm ocean until the turbulence in his soul quieted. He could have stretched out on a beach chair and immersed himself in a novel to quiet the thoughts of his mind. He could have done a hundred things other than engage the reply. Slowly he began to understand that he had not randomly stumbled upon this great need, he had been led there. He had intentionally been shown the desperation and cruelty of poverty beyond anything he could ever have imagined. Elio quieted his heart and lifted his eyes to heaven. "I will build them houses, Lord. I will build them houses."

The wrong turn in the road turned out to be very right. It was the first step to a journey that would bring transformation to thousands of lives and even to the very core of the Sosua region in the Dominican Republic. More than 1300 families now live in neat rows of new homes that dot the countryside in new villages. In the centre of each bustling village sits a church, a school, a medical centre, and other community buildings.

"What are you going to do about it?" has become an incredible story of remarkable change, brought about because one man opened his eyes to see the needs surrounding him and stepped out to do something about it.

As Elio explored just how to go about doing what he now believed God had called him to do, two wise and godly men came alongside him. Rev. Onofrio Miccolis had worked with Elio on several projects throughout many years of friendship and ministry in Canada, and his commitment and partnership with Elio continues to this day.

In order to determine how he might proceed with this promise to build houses, Elio paid a visit to the mayor of Sosua at that time, Mr. Arismendi Medina. Mr. Medina was immediately drawn to the project and began to work devotedly with Elio and Onofrio to combat the devastation brought on by social injustice and cyclical poverty in his country. His intimate knowledge of the Dominican culture and government has proven invaluable.

The processes of purchasing property and applying for development permits carry their own set of challenges in the Dominican Republic. It was through his visit with Mr. Medina that Elio received an obvious miracle, the first of many, he says. He was given a piece of land from the municipality at no cost. Another property, a pig farm, was acquired very near to the donated property and very soon construction of a few small homes began in the periphery of Sosua, right where the praying families from Pastor Reyes Peña's church lived. God had heard and answered their prayers! They told him excitedly of their prayer that God would send a white man from a land far away with a lot of snow, and that his man would help them. It was clear to

them that God had answered their prayers. Elio was certain God would send that man to them but, even though he had provided the first few homes, he was fairly certain he was not that man for the long term. Little did Elio know just where this humble beginning would take him.

Onofrio Miccolis and Elio Madonia have enjoyed a very close working relationship since 1979, but the events of 1988 were totally unplanned by either of them.

It was a year that would forever change the course of both of their lives. Both felt a strong inner compulsion to devote themselves fully to working with those caught in the endless cycle of extreme poverty, the poorest of the poor. Both felt drawn to do similar work but in two different parts of the world, Elio in the Dominican Republic and Onofrio in India. Onofrio began to spend much of his time in India, but the two men stayed in touch, encouraging each other in their difficult, parallel journeys.

When Elio had completed the construction of the first twenty-five homes, he was sure that he had fulfilled his promise to God and that his job was done. However, more people were pleading with him for help. At the same time pressures were mounting in his personal life. He was discouraged. How could he manage his retirement, care for his ailing wife, and meet the needs of so many at the same time? Elio and Lena began to ask God for direction, and soon became united in their agreement to postpone their personal retirement plans with a growing desire to meet the needs as God enabled them. Onofrio felt compelled to help his friend through this difficult season. His lifelong work in television inspired him to use this medium to raise awareness of the plight of the poor living in the Dominican Republic. He and his daughter, a singer, travelled to Sosua with their TV camera and taped the first ever one-hour television program that told the story of the dramatic difference that a 'hand up' had made in the lives of the fortunate few that had received homes, and presented the opportunities and challenges that lay ahead. It sparked interest in the hearts of people in Italy, Canada, and the US, and small groups began to come to Sosua to help. The work had begun and the end is not yet here.

Onofrio understands the plight of the poor. "I myself come from very poor and humble beginnings. I know what it means to have no shoes to go to school, to wear the old clothes of others, even though they were far too large for me. I know what it means to eat the leftovers from the richer people to fill my hungry stomach. When I was only three years old my father left my mother with five children because she had decided to follow Jesus Christ. But God took care of us. I have never forgotten those days and because of that I feel a desire to help others. I had not been able to pursue a proper education,

yet the boy who could not go to school keeps building schools one after the other and distributing scholarships to destitute children. Some have become nurses, teachers, airline personnel, and even medical doctors.

I believe that God can turn our own suffering into a source of strength to help others. I rejoice in the suffering of my childhood. My weaknesses have become my strengths; they motivate me!"

Arismendi Medina is a steadfast and faithful servant of God and his country. He has always been drawn towards helping the impoverished and downtrodden, so he pursued parallel careers as both politician and pastor. While he is a powerful presence in the Dominican Republic, he is also a kind man, a family man, and a man who walks in the strength and confidence of one who knows God intimately.

Working as a politician has given him a voice in raising the level of awareness of the hopeless desperation that is the reality for so many in his country. It has given him a hands-on presence in initiating and expediting change and advancement in this developing country where the political attitude has, until recently, been somewhat resistant to change in this regard. In a recent visit with the president of the country, Elio and Mr. Medina asked him if he thought the government might consider building roads to the newest villages which they have built. It is generally a tedious and often frustrating process to acquire development permits, yet a short while later the roads were built and they were also granted permits to bring city water to these villages.

Mr. Medina sits in several seats of political authority and serves as an advisor to the president. Although this requires much of his time, his devotion to his family, his church and assisting in the leadership of the Samaritan Foundation is unwavering. Over dinner we asked Mr. Medina how he was able to achieve so much. His response was immediate. "We need to do what we can, when we can. We must find what is in our hand and share it. You see, sometimes we have nothing to give, and sometimes we just give nothing. We need to share in the measure that we have been given."

"Find what's in your hand and share it."
-Arismendi Medina

He stopped for a moment. "Small beginnings can lead to great advances. Just begin."

Powerful statements, each one.

Initially Mr. Medina faced many challenges in the development of these villages for the poor. "It was a very, very difficult time," he stated, speaking of the early years. But he remained strong and confident in taking strides to bring balance and awareness of widespread social injustice in their country, regardless of criticism and opposition. As relationships and processes have developed, things have become somewhat easier, but they are certainly not without challenges.

He and his wife, Freda gave sacrificially for many years to provide homes for many families, and and they have been generously blessed in return.

There is an uncommon depth of peace and confidence in the eyes of those who have long walked the journey of witnessing God's provision through difficult times. Eyes that have witnessed this sort of pilgrimage met mine. "God has changed the hearts of the governors of this land," he said.

These three remarkable men began to recognize that this work was not a short-term commitment. They saw that it was to be a long-term venture and as such would require an organizational structure, so they founded the Fundaçion Samaritano in the Dominican Republic. They invited other influential Dominicans to join them in its leadership. The foundation endeavours to help those held captive in the tyranny of generational poverty and social injustice primarily by building homes for them.

Onofrio Miccolis says that there is something mysteriously transformational that happens when people step, for the first time, into the comfort of a home with a bedroom and a simple toilet. Dignity and hope begin to bud. They start dreaming that they can have a better future for themselves and, most of all, for their children because finally they see a ray of hope.

For several years both the Medina and Madonia families supported the building of these homes for the poor. When Elio and Lena's funds neared depletion, save for what they had set aside for their own retirement, they again believed that their work was complete. But God had much more in mind for the poor of the Dominican Republic and for Elio and Lena's retirement years. People from around the globe became aware of the amazing events taking place, and many came to help. When they returned to their homes and shared the stories, it resulted in an even greater influx of those that came to participate in this great adventure. It appeared that God wanted this work to continue for the long term.

Elio has written much more of the early years in his book, *Divine Passion to Help Others*.[4]

Part Two
THE FIRST SEVEN VILLAGES

"Small beginnings can lead to great advances. Just begin."
– Mr. A. Medina

Village #1 – Villa Maranatha

On our first visit to the Dominican Republic in 2006, Elio took us on a truly inspiring tour through all the villages that had been built. As we drove through the countryside in a comfortable, air-conditioned tourist van, we turned into a bustling town. Businesses lined both sides of the busy streets; cars and motorcycles honked and vied for space on the crowded lanes. People called out friendly greetings to each other.

Elio reminded us that it was in the village of Charamicos that the Madonias had been confronted with the squalor of extreme poverty and witnessed for the first time the hopelessness and despair of fellow humans living in sub-human conditions, deprived of all basic necessities of life. It was here that Elio had been able to acquire some land, a small pig farm, and a slaughter house. It was here that the people of Pastor Reyes Peña's church had prayed. It was here that Village #1 was built. They called it Villa Maranatha. The work had begun on two simple streets with twenty-five very basic homes. Before the inauguration services were even held in January of 1990, a school operated by Kids Alive International[5] and a medical clinic managed by Robert and Kelly Williams were already busy hubs within the community. Pastor Reyes Peña has the joy and privilege of leading a thriving congregation in a new church that was built with funds sent from Italy.

Our vehicle turned off the main thoroughfare onto a side street and came to a stop. As we stepped into the hot sunlight, Elio swept wide his arm to present to us the original twenty-five homes that had been built. We were at first admittedly confused. We were looking at a street lined with two-story homes, some painted brightly and with decorative ironwork in their patios and windows. Lovely fences and flowerbeds graced many of the yards. Upon closer inspection we could see the skeleton of the simple home that had originally been granted to them. With a big smile on his face, our driver, Juan, took us to one of these homes. He and his wife had been one of the original recipients. His wife set up a small store in their front room and he bought an old car with the money they had previously needed to pay rent for the mud hovel they lived in. Juan used this old car as a taxi. Eventually he saved enough money to buy a fifteen-seater tourist van and was able to penetrate the tourism industry. He has since purchased a second tourist van. Their two children are now young adults studying at the local university.

Right from the start the recipients of these homes have proven themselves to be industrious and progressive, and Villa Maranatha has become a flourishing community. Today, unless you are familiar with the basic structure of the original homes, you would be hard pressed to find the first streets that were built here. The town now boasts over eight hundred homes and many businesses. More than four hundred worshippers now attend Pastor Reyes Peña's church.

Village #2 – Villa Betania

Shortly after Villa Maranatha was complete, a plot of land only a mile away was purchased and forty-two more homes and a church were built. The children attend school only minutes away in Villa Maranatha.

Village #3 – Villa Emmanuel

As the vision grew, funds and teams came from Northern Europe and Australia. Just a mile from Villa Betania, forty-four homes, complete with electricity and clean water, were built to establish Villa Emmanuel. The church, sponsored and built by Mercy Ships[6] and pastored by Jose Polanco, has become a lively meeting place in this community. The children have access to quality education at schools in both Villa Emmanuel and nearby Villa Maranatha.

"Take the first step in faith. You don't have to see the whole staircase, just take the first step."
– Dr. Martin Luther King, Jr.

Village #4 – Villa Trinidad

In 1997 a fire ripped through a small nearby settlement, igniting the shanties like dry kindling, leaving seventy largely Haitian families homeless and destitute. The Fundaçion Samaritano stepped in to help with the immediate needs of these families and the fourth village, Villa Trinidad, was built. Though the initial homes were very humble, many of the recipients used these as a stepping-stone to improving the lives of their families. Some have added a second story to the basic footprint to make room for businesses on the main floor.

The people of this village have demonstrated a real sense of responsibility and initiative. They established the first Residence Council that is responsible for the management of the affairs of the village. It worked so well that it became a prototype for village governance and administration structure, and is being incorporated in all of the other villages.

Village #5 – Villa Redencion (Redemption)

That same year, Elio purchased another block of land that would provide homes for one hundred and sixty-three more families of both Dominican and Haitian descent who were living in unimaginable deprivation. The board's plan was to build homes for these families immediately but because of difficulties in acquiring permits it took four years to complete this new village. It was the largest village built to this point. Through a grant from the Canadian government, a school was built to accommodate three hundred students. An organization called New Mission[7] took on the responsibility to sponsor each of the students and manage the school. Initially a Spanish church was constructed, and soon afterward a large donation was received designated for the construction of a Creole church so that the Haitians could worship in their own language.

Village #6 – Villa Ascension

There is an idyllic feel to the drive into Villa Ascension. Perhaps it is the large green fields on which children run and play. Perhaps it is the brightly painted walls of the community centre boldly splashed with giant sunflowers, or it might be the large central green area where banana plants and other fruits and vegetables surround the gazebo that sits in the centre of town that create a vibrant, yet tranquil welcome.

In one building some of the women are busy making crafts for sale at the market while others are intent on the mothering and nutrition course they are taking. Just a few steps down the road at the business centre, local vendors, tradesmen, and craftsmen sell their wares or talents. It began as a micro finance enterprise, but the

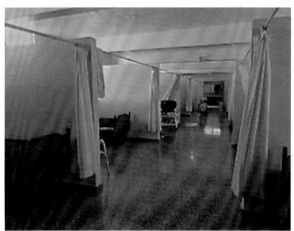

entrepreneurs now work independently, offering services such as small engine repair, bicycle repair, and original artwork, to name a few. An audio-visual library and a computer training facility offer further educational opportunities for adults. The Fundaçion Samaritano built a woodworking shop here, not only to train local people with a trade, but also to manufacture the growing number of windows, doors and other building components that were needed for their projects.

There is something very special about Villa Ascension. It certainly merits a moment to stop to take note of the dramatic transformation that has taken place in a mature village, where residents have come into their stride as contributing members of society.

My moment of reverie is interrupted by voices of children reciting their schoolwork through the open windows of the school. Moments later the children spill out into the much-loved playground. Those that don't rush to greet us run to the open field for a game of soccer or to test their skills at the basketball court.

A bus rumbles into town, bringing many of the residents home at the end of their work day.

The people of Villa Ascension did not always enjoy such an opportunity rich environment. Hundreds of Haitian, Haitian Dominican, and Dominican families lived in over crowded and deplorable conditions in the isolated, low-lying settlement of Caraballo in the abandoned sugar cane fields outside of Montellano. It is an area that is prone to frequent flooding. Yet in spite of the abundance of water the people still had no access to clean drinking water, and education was a luxury beyond their reach. Racial tensions created an atmosphere of fear and violence.

In 2002, twenty-one acres of land was acquired in nearby Montellano, and in 2003 construction of the Village of Ascension began on this site.

We have often heard the African adage that it takes a whole village to raise a child. In the Dominican we have witnessed that it takes a whole world of caring people to create a village. A group of Italian donors built a clinic and donated an ambulance for this new village. Canadian groups collected funds for the construction of a large church and provided the medical equipment needed in the clinic. An American organization provided money for the first eighty houses and built several wells. This water served the community during the building process, however when the residents came to live in the village the water supply was insufficient. Two 20,000-gallon reservoirs were built and water is pumped two miles from the Puerto Plata Aqueducts.

Groups and individuals[8] from England, Canada, and the US all combined their efforts to build the remaining houses, a first-rate school, a library, and a kindergarten. Kids Alive International continues to provide quality education to the children of the village.

Dr. Bob and Jana Amelingmeier of Dominican Crossroads[9] officially joined efforts with Fundaçion Samaritano at the inception of Ascension and have been key leaders in the community since that time. Prior to this, the dynamic couple lived in Haiti, working with orphans and looking after the medical needs of the sick. During a season of uprising, the horrific scenes of violence and torture playing out all around them proved to be too traumatic and dangerous for this couple and their seven children. They lived without electricity, running water and phone services, and many nights Dr. Bob was not able to make it home because of danger in the streets. For the sake of their family, they moved to the Dominican Republic to continue their work with the Haitians on that side of the border. Their contributions towards the availability and advancement of quality medical care are immeasurable. Their love and concern for the poor, the sick, and the homeless are evidenced in their programs that bring food, medical aid, and other necessities to the dumps and to the slums.

Dr. Bob has started a Sunday school in Ascension, and Jana has seen the benefits of a retreat centre that they recently established to welcome those who are weary and need refreshing.

In the end, 263 families from among the poorest of the poor have received keys to safe, dry homes. The vibrancy of the village attests to the fact that these people have risen to grasp the opportunities offered them. They have made their houses homes, and their village a community.

Village #7 – Villa Nazareth

The village of Nazareth, very near Betania, Trinidad, and Redencion is situated on a beautiful hillside. Two sparkling clean and well-maintained buildings at the entrance to the village house the Dr. Phyllis Callahan Christian School and Danica's Dream Medical Outreach.

Philip and Donna Williams had never been on an international holiday. They came to the Dominican Republic with friends just when Villa Nazareth was in its initial stages. The desperate need of the people gripped their hearts, and an inner compulsion urged them to come and make a difference. Within six months they had sold their home in Canada and were back in Nazareth. They founded an organization called Servant's Heart[10], and have made a huge impact on the health and welfare of people in the villages through their two medical clinics. Their compassion for those seemingly forgotten in the outlying regions led them to build a mobile medical

clinic which regularly visits those who have no access to medical care.

An enthusiastic passion for quality education at the school in Nazareth is not only taught, but caught. Dr. Kim and Josie Pensinger came to the Dominican Republic from the U.S. with a deep-seated desire to provide quality education for those who have no opportunity to go to school. It is impossible to grow beyond their present circumstances without the advantage of an education. Together they established Dominican Advance[11] and with the help of dedicated and competent principal, Dr. Yamilka Estrada the next generation is seeing opportunities that their parents only dreamed of. Dr. Estrada initially worked as a lawyer, but she was so impressed with the opportunities being presented to the illiterate children in her country that she went back to university to become a teacher.

We stop for a quick visit in a nearby home. Carmen and her husband have ten children. He is a truck driver. His salary does not begin to cover the needs of a family of this size, so in his travels he gleans fields for leftover produce to feed their family. Though the fire is burning in her outdoor kitchen, there is no food to be seen and the noon hour sun is high in the sky. She doesn't know when her husband will be home. Sometimes he is gone for a couple of days and sometimes for two weeks. Sometimes he brings mangoes or plantain, and sometimes, she looks away, sometimes nothing. Yesterday a neighbour had given them some sweet potatoes, so they had eaten. Today, well, today she hopes her husband will come home with food. Her health is not good and she has difficulty walking, but she isn't able to afford the medication that she needs to address a kidney condition.

In spite of the difficult financial situation they find themselves in, her face glows with an inner contentment and love for her family. The inner glow emanates from a deep faith in the God of the Bible. She finds no greater joy than sharing the joy she has with her neighbours.

Her eyes light up as she tells us about her children. They are all in school. The teachers say that their Maria is brilliant and she wants to be a doctor. One of her sons is very talented in their national sport, baseball. He shyly slides closer to me with his notebook in his hand and says that he also likes to study.

On our way out of the village we stop at the grocery kiosk. Whether her husband comes home or not, today they will eat.

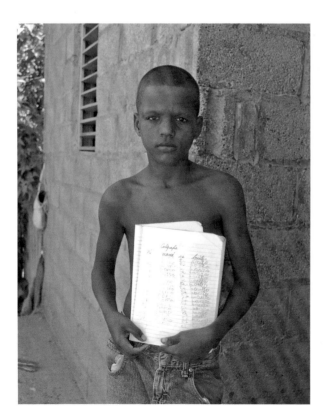

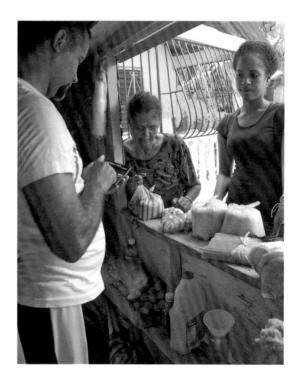

Part Three

AN EXPLOSION OF HELP

"Chance encounters, words spoken in passing, are they mere coincidence, or might they be servants of divine appointment, gateways to our destiny, invitations to the working of the Supernatural?"

– Dori Sawatzky

In 2006 there was a veritable flood of people who came to help. More property was purchased by the foundation and additional lands were donated. More teams arrived from around the world, sometimes two or even three at a time. Some came to build, some to paint, some to teach, and some to provide finances or encouragement. This was also the year that my husband, Ben Sawatzky and I had the privilege of stepping into this incredible story. Each team member, every volunteer that came to help became aware that there was a specific purpose for their presence in the Dominican Republic. Their lives were deeply impacted by the realization that their ordinary talents and contributions were vital cogs in the wheels of change. They had become part of the solution; they had become world changers. Faceless statistics turned into personal relationships.

For three men, there was a deeper, long-term connection that was to happen. With the increasing administrative requirements and growing international attention, it became apparent that it was time to establish a Canadian arm of the foundation with its own board of directors. The Samaritan Foundation was established and

these three men, Tore Stautland, Ben Sawatzky, and Phil Donne were asked by Elio Madonia and Onofrio Miccolis to join them to form the board for this new foundation.

Tore Stautland, a Canadian television producer, is also a pastor and passionate humanitarian. Through his relationship with several large international pharmaceutical and medical supply companies he is able to ship medicines, hospital equipment, supplements and other necessities to established distribution centres around the globe. It was through a chance encounter that Tore and his wife, Julie, found themselves chatting with Elio's brother. The topic turned to the

needs of those living in poverty stricken countries and Tore spoke about their medical distribution opportunities, to which Elio's brother suggested that they might consider sending medical aid to his brother in the Dominican Republic. Connections were made and soon after four pallets of hospital supplies and various medications were placed in containers and shipped to Sosua. As is his practice, Tore followed the shipment to make a personal visit and to establish relationships. Tore and his family have a special interest in the Dominican Republic. They have long sponsored a child named Luz Esther through Compassion Canada[12], and wanted very much to meet her. He mentioned this to Elio, but was very doubtful that he would be able to help them; she lived in such a remote and obscure little village named Betania. As it happened, Elio knew her well. He proceeded to tell Tore that the Samaritan Foundation had presented her family with their first house in Villa Betania. The school Luz Esther attends was built by friends of the foundation. He was happy to take Tore and Julie to meet their sponsored daughter.

As Elio showed Tore the work and shared his philosophy of ministry, their hearts bonded in the call to help the poor. In time Tore was asked to become a member of the board of directors. He says, "It is almost impossible to take in the depth of genuine affliction and not feel completely overwhelmed and almost helpless to make a difference. Sometimes the real problems are hidden behind a veil that conceals conflicting agendas and supply chain corruption. The global maternal instinct is strong when it is energized by the haunting cries of the world's most desperate children. But we are all children in need and responsible to do our part in meeting such need."

When Tore returned to Canada, he enthusiastically shared the story of the developments in the Dominican Republic with us. We were immediately intrigued and soon traveled to the Dominican to see the work first hand. Ben and Elio walked the land and heard each other's hearts. After a period of time, Elio asked Ben if he

would consider joining them in the leadership of the Samaritan Foundation.

Ben agreed and says that, "It is a privilege to walk alongside these men, trying to keep pace with the mighty work of God in lifting those entrenched in the clutches of cyclical poverty to a place of hope for the future."

Phil Donne had been observing the growing impact of the Samaritan Foundation from a unique perspective of a son-in-law. He is married to Elio and Lena's daughter, Lucy.

"Each time I would go to volunteer, be it for a few days or a week, I felt that there was perhaps more that I could do than just provide funds and the odd brick moving job." It was on one of these volunteer trips that he and two of his colleagues heard about the desire to provide villagers with basic skills to improve their employment opportunities. They felt that this was an area where they might be able to add value, and through Village Bridge[13] provided funds that would assist in establishing what was to become a vocational training centre. They continue to support initiatives that will help the village residents find their way out of poverty and lead the way towards economic sustainability. "The nudge to become involved began at a volunteer level and eventually the notion that we could do more came through," says Phil. Many, many improvements have been made since that first encounter and yet there is still so much to be done.

As the work grew, it became evident that a full time director was needed. The board began to pray.

John and Jane Huizinga were living a very comfortable life in Ontario, Canada. They knew that someday they would like to go work in missions somewhere, but right now times were very good where they were. He loved his work and had attained the highest managerial position in the company he worked for.

John was introduced to the developmental work of the Samaritan Foundation on a three-day

work mission in Villa Ascension when he was in the Dominican Republic visiting his son, who was a student there. "It was in Villa Ascension that I felt God touch my heart, tap me on the shoulder, and tell me that this was my new job. It pretty well scared me to death because this wasn't the place I had in mind for missions, and it certainly wasn't the time I would choose. I always knew God had a sense of humor, but this wasn't funny at all!" He made a deal with God that he was sure he would win. He said, "Lord, I'll go, but you'll have to convince my wife, Jane, of it too." Three years later they were in the Dominican working with the Samaritan Foundation.

The extreme challenges and steep learning curve have been profound instruments of change and growth in their lives. "I often wonder why God chose Jane and me to fill this position. We don't have any special education. We have stumbled many times but God has always picked us back up, dusted us off, and got us going again. Sometimes a little battered, a little hurt, and even a little bruised, but never destroyed. The years we have served here have been the very best and the very toughest years in our life together. God has stretched our faith and trust in Him beyond our wildest imaginings and yet He has never let us down or broken us in two. We both have said that we would never trade these five years in the Dominican Republic for any of the previous five years in our lives." The weight of leadership and the call to pioneer are never easy, yet the personal and spiritual benefits far outweigh the cost.

One can only imagine that as word spread that there were free houses to be had for those in desperate need, the leadership at the Samaritan Foundation were highly sought after! In anticipation of this, the Fundaçion Samaritano board set up qualifying criteria both in relation to the character of the recipient, and also in consideration of the types of individuals that would be needed for the organization and function of a new village. A good cross section of people would be required. One could not simply build replacement homes for the intended recipients because they did not own the land or shacks where they were living. Land needed to first be purchased on which to build new homes. Before a home could be built, the preparatory work of government permits, land purchases, availability of clean drinking water, and town planning all needed to be addressed.

While it remains a priority that the poorest of the poor are granted safe and secure homes, some recipients were chosen because of their leadership capabilities or their hard work ethic. Some are single parents and some are seniors who have no one to take care of them. Each recipient is required to dig a hole for a septic tank for the home that they will live in. Title to the home is not immediately granted. For five years the resident must 'earn' the right to the title of the home by keeping it clean, planting flowers and vegetables in their small plots, and by being helpful and contributing members of their new society. After five years the title is given to the woman of the home because, in the event that she should be deserted, it is the custom that the children stay with their mother, and they would then have the security of a home of their own.

There is a huge benefit in moving people out of a physical place of hopelessness and transplanting them into a place of new beginnings; a new home, a new town, new neighbours; a place with structure, civic expectation, and hope.

While there are countries that have more widespread poverty and more deplorable living conditions, the social and political climate in the Dominican Republic provides a setting that makes it ripe for transformation. That transformation is happening not only in the landscape of the country, but in the very hearts of the people. On a clear day, if your airline flies along the Sosua coastline, you will see more than 1300 homes tucked amongst the greenery of the treetops. Each one is a testament to the advancement towards breaking the cycle of generational poverty one person, one family, and one home at a time.

Part Four

A TRUE STORY OF TRANSFORMATION

"Find what's in your hand and share it."

-Arismendi Medina

Village #8 – Los Algodones
and Villa Esperanza

While each village and each household bears witness to the provision of God and the goodness and generosity of so many, Los Algadones/Villa Esperanza is a story of new beginnings and budding hope like we have never seen elsewhere.

Several years ago a group from Mission Direct,[8] England, was working at the construction of the town of Villa Ascension and they took a day to visit some of the neighbouring shanty towns to distribute medicines, food, clothes, and educational and personal supplies. On this particular day they stopped in the village of Los Algodones. About two hundred families, mostly Haitian, lived in squalid, sub-human conditions. Children played or wandered about aimlessly. There was a small public school for them within walking distance, but the program was very poor and the teachers showed up inconsistently. The children were dusty and dirty. Raw sewage ran openly in the narrow pathways between the crowded rows of houses. Live electrical wires flapped loosely in the breeze. A sense of hopelessness hung like oppression over the shanty town. There was no source of potable water except for the water truck that came by regularly. Since they had little or no money, water was a luxury they could ill afford. There was a murky pool of water at the bottom of a hillside nearby that the waste washed into from the village and from the nearby farmer's cattle fields. This is where many of the villagers did their laundry, bathed, and many drank from. Child mortality rates were high. Illness was rampant.

The team members' hearts ached for these people and they begged the Samaritan Foundation to find a way for these people to get water, while they committed to do all they could to raise funds for a school for the children. Elio expended a great deal of energy to attempt to bring water to Los Algodones.

Because of the deep divide between the Haitians and the Dominicans in this country, Elio soon found that it would take a miracle for the water department to grant them a permit to help bring water to this village.

Six months passed with no headway. Then one day a significant introduction was made. Elio's good friend, Don Juan Paliza introduced him to Dr. Umbert Hart. Dr. Hart was Dominican born and educated but had moved to the United States and had become a doctor of some renown. He had returned to his homeland for retirement and Don Juan Paliza was showing him the tremendous changes that the Samaritan Foundation was bringing to the Dominican

Republic. He explained that they wanted to build a school for the children and a village for the families but they could not get a permit to bring water up to the village in order to be granted a permit to build a school. You cannot have a school without water. Dr. Hart's passion and influence quickly swayed those in authority and in a few days permission was granted to bring water to the area of Los Algodones. Miraculously the money needed for construction materialized and the mile long pipeline was installed.

During the intervening months, a team from Spruceland Millworks in Alberta, Canada,[14] had sponsored and erected a 90,000-liter water reservoir in anticipation of this day. We had the privilege of watching with excited expectation as the tap was turned on for the first time. Fresh, clean water sputtered, then burst out of the two-inch pipe.

Oh! What joy! What celebration and laughter! The people lined up with their buckets and pails. Children hopped from one foot to another. Some jumped right under the cold, clean water, letting it run over their dusty bodies and clothing, opening their mouths wide to drink. One grandmother with tears in her eyes quietly told us that this was the first time she had seen clean water in sixty years. She was raising five grandchildren.

True to their word, Mission Direct returned with funds to purchase the land and construct a school across the street from the slums of

Los Algodones. Permits were granted, not only to build the school, but also a church and a medical centre. International Needs Networks[15] undertook the administration of the school. A group from Ontario, Canada, came to build the Dr. Umbert Hart medical clinic and did much to improve the lives of the people in Los Algodones. The clinic is managed and operated by Rob and Tina Ianonne, who work very closely with the Samaritan Foundation. A local doctor and nurse provide the medical expertise needed to meet the many demands.

The Ministry of Tourism, however, was still refusing to grant permits to build houses. At the same time, Elio received a commitment that would supply all the lumber required for construction for this village and for all future projects of the Samaritan Foundation. A flow of containers filled with lumber began to arrive regularly from the northern ports of Canada. When the owners of the shipping company, Doug and Denise Romanuk, learned the purpose of the lumber shipments, they donated the cost of the shipments themselves.

Though lumber was piling up and construction was at a standstill, God was still on the move, and so were Elio and his team. Hundreds of impoverished families were waiting for homes. Unable to move ahead, they located another beautiful property to build the ninth village, but the high price tag made it prohibitive to

them. Along came Archie Robertson, president of Home Equity Investments Rewards Inc., and twenty-five of his associates. They walked the proposed site and Archie felt an inner nudge to provide the funds to help. Without hesitation he promised to provide the means to purchase the property and secured the land with a deposit on the spot. This became the site for village number nine.

This, however, was not the end of the story of Los Algodones. Lucy, a Dominican pastor from the other side of the island, heard of the work of the Samaritan Foundation and came to see the villages. She was appalled at the deplorable conditions that these people were forced to live in, and could not understand how permits could be withheld for the gift of free housing to those in such evident need. Lucy was not without connections.

Two weeks later Lucy returned with Mr. Freddy Veragoiko, the most famous television host in the Dominican Republic. Tears came to Freddy's eyes as he witnessed the filth and squalor of the living conditions, the desperation and hopelessness in the eyes of those living in his own country. His cameramen captured it well. Freddy featured Elio and the urgent need of those living in their own backyard, and told how foreigners from other countries desired to build homes for these people. Within two weeks permits were granted to build the houses in the new town that would replace Los Algadones. They named it Esperanza, which means hope.

The residents were given the news that a new village with 260 homes would be built across the street from Los Algodones. Those who lived responsibly, were good to their families and neighbours, and who kept their current places clean, would be the first to be considered.

This infusion of hope brought astounding transformation even before the first home was built. Immediately the atmosphere in the village improved. There was a new light in the eyes of the people. A sense of expectation brought with it a new respect for both property and the people around them.

Ernie and Helen Kehler, the owners of Greenvalley Equipment, Inc. in southern Manitoba, sat in the company coffee room and listened as one of their employees, Brian Dueck, told of the exciting work that some of his family members were involved with in the Dominican Republic. He told how a company in Alberta was matching funds that their employees donated, to help build houses and community buildings for the impoverished. Not only could the employees donate a portion of their earnings, but many of them actually went down on work teams organized by their employer. The leadership at Greenvalley Equipment not only caught his enthusiasm, they caught the vision. Managers Ryan Toews and Curtis Sanjenko contacted Spruceland Millworks

and very soon gave their employees the same opportunity. They too, could make contributions through payroll deductions that the company would match. They too, began to bring work teams to the Dominican. The owners and staff at Greenvalley Equipment have truly been impacted by being instruments of change and development in the Dominican. Their commitment to something bigger than themselves, bigger than their jobs, has brought them closer as a team. Since that initial conversation, Greenvalley has sponsored 52 homes in Esperanza. Their generosity has also been felt in other villages with the donations of a medical centre, a playground, a Bobcat, and an infusion of resources in the construction of an adult vocational training centre.

Something magical seems to happen inside our human hearts when we see the needs around us and reach out to give of ourselves and of what we have to help others. We lose a piece of our hearts in the process and in turn our hearts are forever enriched by the memories of those we have helped. Because each individual and each organization played their role, the quality of life for the residents of Los Algadones has been transformed from one of a hopeless and forgotten existence to one of opportunity and anticipation.

A couple of years later, after several of the villagers had received homes in Esperanza, we again walked through Los Algodones. As new

homes were built, the old ones were torn down, leaving small empty lots. Only a year or two earlier, children had run through the raw sewage where live electrical wires dangled threateningly. Now children's laughter rang from these small lots. These squares of empty space not only let more sunlight into the cramped quarters, but they were swept clean and the children used them as play spaces.

Today, in 2013, you can no longer visit the village of Los Algodones. Only three or four of the original structures remain. You can, however, visit the thriving town of Esperanza directly across the street. Children's voices emanate from school classrooms and voices raised in praise and singing float through the church windows. You will see people lined up at the clinic door, thankful for medical help that is so accessible and affordable. In the playground you might find the boys' soccer team preparing for their next tournament. Residents are hard at work in the jewelry enterprise that ships jewelry to many countries around the world. Parents and grand-parents industriously sweep their patios and wash down the streets and sidewalks in front of their homes. Some have painted beautiful murals on the outside walls. Sickness and mortality rates have improved substantially.

In spite of the improvement in their circum-stances, poverty still breathes its worrisome lament. "Will we have food for tomorrow? Will I find work tomorrow?" John Huizinga, the Director of Samaritan Foundation, is quick to remind visiting teams, "Remember, giving them a home has merely lifted them from abject poverty into extreme poverty; yet here they have some opportunities they never had before."

A young boy runs up to me with a notebook in his hand. "What is your name?" he asks, proud to use the English he has learned in school. "My name is Dori. What is yours?" He jabs with his fingers at the notebook and pen in my hands. "Write," he instructs. I write my name at the top. He takes the notebook and writes his name for me. A crowd of children gathers and an elderly man walks slowly to the young boy beside me. He doesn't immediately notice his grandfather. He is busy pointing to each of his friends and proudly writing their names in my notebook. His grandfather puts his hand on his grandson's shoulder with evident pride and joy on his face. In Creole, interspersed with Spanish, he looks us in the eyes and says, "I tell him every day he must do well in school." His own opportunities for lit-eracy are past but the hope and pride that he felt for his grandson needs no interpreter.

On this particular day, a team from Mission Direct is hard at work painting doors and windows, when the children allow them to! Their love for the people and their devotion to the project is evident in everything they do. Each year they send several teams to bring encouragement and assistance to the building projects that are underway. Claire Hodgson from England is the Dominican Director of Mission Direct and lives in Sosua for nine to ten months of the year. She came on her first visit to the Dominican Republic in 2009 and knew immediately that it was right for her to be here. Claire's enthusiasm is contagious and it is evident by the swarm of children and youth constantly crowding around her that she is well loved by the community.

Josh Sawatzky organizes the teams that come to the Dominican through Spruceland Millworks and its associates. During the winter of 2011, after a long day's work in the blistering heat with the team, the refreshing waters of the ocean were beckoning powerfully. As he was about to dip his feet into the water, one of the hotel scuba instructors called out to him. "Hey, are you Josh Sawatzky?" Josh affirmed that he was. "Thank you, thank you, thank you! My name is Xavier Luckny and I received one of the homes in Esperenza. I have a wonderful wife and two beautiful children. I wanted to tell you how much this has changed our lives. Because I received a home I was able to put my salary towards a motorcycle." He explained that this not only allowed him to get to work without paying exorbitant taxi fares, but it also allowed him to earn extra money by using it as a moto-taxi.

He communicates effortlessly in English, Spanish, and French. "Russian is next," he says, anticipation sparkling in his eyes. When we asked where and how he learned all these languages so quickly, his instant reply was, "From God." He was always asking people for books, even as a child in Haiti, and he very quickly just knew what the foreign languages meant.

Xavier Luckny is a man driven to succeed. After high school he moved to the Dominican from Haiti, hoping for a better life. It was not to be, at least not at first. He ended up in the slums of Los Algodones and lived for one and a half years with one pair of pants and two t-shirts. He worked long days as a landscaper for $8.00 a day, but that money was all eaten up with transportation to get to work and for rent for a dwelling that could never qualify as a home. He hung his head; sad memories clouded his eyes. "But," he said as he looked up, "I never gave up hope. And I always continued to improve myself in any and every way I could. I have learned a lot." It seems fitting that he and his family received a home in the village whose name means Hope.

In 2007 Lois Jacobs came to Esperanza with a church team from Texas to help with the construction of the village. In her heart she knew there must be something more that she could do to help. She considered the talents that she had in jewelry making and formulated a plan. The next year she returned. She taught some of the residents how to make beautiful jewelry by recycling paper and other scraps. She sponsored a building for their budding venture and assisted them in establishing Recycle H. O. P. E. – Helping Other People Eat.[16] People from around the globe can now assist in providing jobs and ultimately in helping other people eat by purchasing jewelry from Recycle H. O. P. E. on their website. Xavier Luckny is the manager of this establishment when he is not teaching scuba diving at a local resort.

The gift of generosity has not been lost on this industrious group of people. Out of their profits they have begun a program of bringing Christmas food hampers to the seniors in their village. This past Christmas they distributed forty-nine hampers, this from a group of people who do not have food for their families every day.

Part Five

GROWTH AND OPPORTUNITY

"Now all glory to God, who is able, through His mighty power at work within us, to accomplish infinitely more than we can ask or think."
– Ephesians 3:20

Village #9 – Villa Spruceland
Paraiso (Paradise)

Sometimes the practice of listening causes one to question their hearing.

Elio could not wait to show Ben Sawatzky the land that Archie Robertson had purchased for a new village. The two men walked the length and width of the property, imagining, calculating, dreaming, and admiring the view of the distant ocean. Along with community buildings, they estimated approximately two hundred families could receive homes. As they walked and talked, Ben heard a parallel quiet whisper in his soul. "I would like you to commit to building this village." He listened more intently to Elio but the whisper was not to be ignored.

A tumultuous inner conversation ensued. The timing was not good. The lumber industry had been attacked and almost decimated at every turn for the previous two years, and Spruceland Millworks, the source of his provision, is a lumber company. In addition to this the financial markets had crashed, leaving his investment portfolio crippled. How could he pledge to build a village when he was not even sure that the business he co-owned with his brother, Willy, would survive the current crisis? How could he ask his business partners to join him in this commitment? How could he raise the hopes of so many if he couldn't follow through with his promise? He shared his conflicted feelings with me, his wife, bringing us to our knees to listen for the answer. The whisper became a conviction. The questions, still unanswered, were met with a peace and calm of the soul. We stepped out in faith and committed to Elio and the board that all two hundred homes would be paid for.

Coming from a conservative religious background, much attention had been given to the biblical principle that one should not let their left hand know what their right hand is doing. Gifts given to God's work were private, between the giver and God. Again, the whisper came. "Share the journey. Invite others to be part of the blessing. Invite your partners, invite your employees, invite your friends."

At the following company Christmas party the staff were shown a slideshow of the humanitarian opportunities that the company had supported because of profits gained through the employees' hard work and dedication. Future plans were presented and a very short, no-pressure opportunity was given to the staff to become involved. An hour of donated overtime per pay cheque, after a two-year period, would buy a house for a family in need. They could contribute through payroll deductions, which the family foundation would match. Seventy-six percent of the employees immediately jumped at the chance. Shortly after that the company began to organize work trips for employees, family, and friends. Other organizations caught the vision and have presented their employees with the same chance to become involved with the Samaritan Foundation. In the end, staff, family, and friends of the foundation contributed fully half of the project costs.

Work began immediately and within three years 206 families had received keys to safe and secure dwellings that they call home.

In the early stages of the development of the village, a church, a school, a children's centre, and a medical centre were constructed.

Dr. Kim and Josie Pensinger with Dominican Advance were operating the school and sponsorship program in Villa Nazareth efficiently and with great success. It seemed a natural fit for them to expand their work into Paradise and they were happy to do so. Currently the school offers kindergarten to grade six with plans to expand to grade eight. Student outcomes are evidence of quality education, and the enthusiastic and positive attitudes of the teachers attest to an atmosphere based on sound philosophies and loving administration.

The Pensingers, too, had a listening story to share. They had served several years as

missionaries, but had moved back home to the U.S. and had settled in quite nicely to take care of their aging parents, a noble call. When they heard of the new villages that were being built by the Samaritan Foundation, Josie felt a tug within her. "We could go." The thought quickly transferred to a prayer, "But God, you would need to tell my husband, because we really are committed here." Her husband, Kim, felt the same inner compulsion. A short time later he brought up the subject and looked Josie straight in the eye saying, "We need to go."

When the school opened its doors it became apparent that many of the students were irritated, lackluster, and couldn't seem to focus.

Teacher Delvina Plantinas noticed that six year old Eudis was not feeling well. As the days progressed, he was becoming increasingly weak. His sister was also very weak, and one morning she walked up to the teacher's desk, slumped over, and fainted. The teacher and Josie went to visit their mother to see what the problems were and to see if they could help. When they asked her why she was sending her boy to school when he was clearly very ill, she responded that it was the only place that he could eat. Eudis was taken to the clinic and was kept there for two days. He suffered from dehydration, malnutrition, anemia, and the onset of kidney disease.

Though they provided some food at the school, it was evident right from the start that they would need to incorporate a comprehensive nutrition program. They developed the *NutriNiños – Every Child, Every Day* school nutrition program. "If we are requiring them to concentrate and do their best in school, at least we can see to it that they're properly fed when they come," said Josie Pensinger.

The *NutriNiños* program has resulted in the improvement in the general health of the children. Academic performance has improved, attention spans have increased, and respect in the classroom has shown a marked improvement. Another benefit that teachers noticed is the children's increase in energy. Some children who just sat during recess are now playing and interacting with their peers on the playground.

Delvina Plantinas says, "I know I was meant to be a teacher. It's not only about teaching them to read and write, but about showing love and being sensitive to their needs."

She tells us about nine-year-old Luis, a student that manifested extremely violent behaviour, especially towards the girls. He could not read or write and he did not want to be in school. Delvina requested a meeting with his mother, who began to share that there was a lot of violence in the home and he was witnessing this. This was normal behaviour for him.

Delvina began to spend more time with Luis, lovingly sharing with him the importance of education and of being kind. "I don't know how it happened but he began to gravitate towards me. His attitude began to change. I've taught him how to read." He is always showing her his work and wants to know if he's doing it right. Aggressive behaviour toward girls changed, especially toward his sisters at home. His mom says, "He's not like that anymore – and he was constantly beating them up!"

Recently his mom came up to Delvina and enveloped her in a big hug, thanking her for the huge change that had come about in her son and in their family.

Delvina added pensively, "I've seen poverty, not to do with the outward, economic situation of people. I have seen their inner needs up close, and that changed my heart." When she sees how much change she can make in the lives of others by being a teacher, she wants to be the president of the country so that she can help all the people!

Jim and Debra Tunnycliff are the pastors of the church in Paradise. What a celebration was held that first Sunday morning when Jim and Debra arrived and the people gathered together to thank God for all He had done for them. The Tunnycliff's feel a deep desire to help break the chains of poverty in this area of the Dominican Republic. They understand the importance of a strong sense of community and how it brings significant value to the lives of people as they gather and engage together.

Over dinner he tells us of the changes he has seen in the hearts of the people who come to church and who learn of God's love for them. Their hearts are filled with gratitude. He sees the great desperation of the poor on one hand, and on the other he sees the magnificent love of God expressed through the many who give of themselves to build the villages. He is deeply aware of the greatness of God. With deep conviction he states how very much he and Debra are aware that Jesus is needed to span the abyss of soul poverty and to heal the brokenness in the lives of all of us.

Jim says with a smile, "We are giving, yet receiving so much more." Debra has noticed that, in seeking to bring change around them, they themselves have been changed. "With God all things are possible. My faith is through the roof!"

Faith plays a large part in many of the villager's hearts and lives. Besides the village churches, the people have begun to gather in outdoor sanctuaries in a nearby forest and under a huge bamboo tree in the garden that they have designated as a place of prayer. These people meet daily to express their gratitude to a loving God and to present to Him the burdens they still carry.

Rob and Tina Ianonne of Willing Servants[17] manage the clinics in Esperanza and Paradise. Tina works at the clinic full time and Rob helps when he is not hosting visiting teams. On any

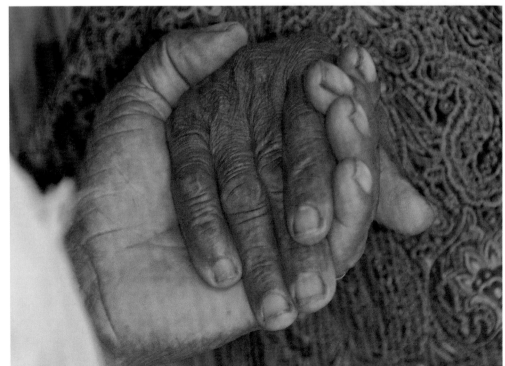

weekday morning when Tina opens the door to the medical clinic, the chairs in the waiting room fill up quickly. Dedicated staff handle the day-to-day ailments and dispense Tylenol, vitamins, and antibiotics. A couple of times a week Dr. Emmanuel Lambert comes to see those that may have more significant medical needs. This vital role is much appreciated by the people of the village and often serious illnesses are warded off through early intervention and education.

Behind the medical centre in Paradise is a small seniors' complex.

Ramon Dias and Ostelia Lopez have spent their entire lives in less than desirable circumstances. Now in their old age, they are thrilled with a safe, clean single room apartment with the clinic next door and the community park just steps from their front door. They have endured much hardship in decades of marriage. When asked, "What has changed the most for you, living here now?", the woman's simple reply was revealing. "I am no longer afraid when it rains." One can only imagine the fear this woman must have suffered all those years when they lived along the edge of the river. Every dark cloud, every raindrop could mean a rising and raging river. Much has been lost to the river many times over. Her relief was obvious in her huge smile and her warm hug. Their new comfort was truly valued.

When all the buildings in the village were complete, Paradise hummed with excitement, life, and positivity. Children ran happily to school, books in hand, uniforms neat and clean. A constant stream of moto-taxis carried people to work, to look for work, or just to take care of the business of the day. While it was evident that the wheels of transformation had begun to turn, the work was not complete. The next generation would have many opportunities open to them by the time they grew up, but the opportunities for their parents, many of them still in their thirties, had not changed. They now had a roof over their heads, but they still faced a lifetime of unemployment, or at best in temporary day jobs where they were drastically underpaid because they lacked the education or skills to improve their prospects. In seeking to advance the progress of sustainable economic development, the board decided to build a vocational training centre.

They set out to determine which marketable skills might best assist the adults in the area, and to find funding partners. It was resolved that they would build a vocational training centre with faculties in woodworking, agriculture, adult literacy, hair design & barbering, sewing & tailoring, and plumbing & electrical and small engine repair.

Jim and Debra Tunnycliff, the local pastors, were ecstatic when they heard of these developments. The Tunnycliffs had a vision for not only building faith among the people here but also of giving them the opportunity to develop marketable skills as well. It had long been in their hearts to begin and to manage such a program, but the demands of church life left them with little time or energy to put their dream into motion. With the board leading the way they very quickly stepped into their dream. They presented the plans to the government officials who not only granted them a permit to build, but through their Infotep program also provided government-approved curriculum along with qualified teachers whose salaries are paid for by the government. Furthermore, the certificates of graduation are valid in fourteen Caribbean and Latin American countries. The future holds the promise of hope not only for the next generation but for this current generation of adults as well.

> "Now all glory to God, who is able, through His mighty power at work within us,
> to accomplish infinitely more than we can ask or think!"
> – Ephesians 3:20 New Living Translation.

The Faculty of Woodworking

Just shy of the border to the Northwest Territories in Canada rests the small town of LaCrete, Alberta. Through conversations with his friends in the lumber industry, local business-man John Unger became aware of the develop-ment of a woodworking shop in Paradise in the Dominican Republic. He and his wife, Ruth, were both intrigued. They traveled to see the project and their hearts were moved with compassion as they witnessed the extreme difficulties the people face daily in their quest for the very basic necessities of life. They jumped at the chance of co-sponsoring the woodworking project. The opportunities for learning a marketable skill impacts so many of the adults in the village, among them the instructor at the woodworking shop, Byrvens Pierre.

Byrvens quoted this Bible verse to us. "For I know the plans I have for you, says the Lord, plans to prosper you and bring you good success." Jeremiah 29:11

Byrvens has seen God's evident hand in the fulfillment of this promise in his life. His father and two brothers are pastors in his homeland of Haiti, and Byrvens was involved in leadership in the church from a young age. Although only two or three out of ten applicants in Haiti are accepted into university each year, Byrvens was one of those selected. He studied woodworking

44

for three years, "but it was only book learning and not hands-on training." Political unrest in 2005 made it extremely dangerous for him to continue studying, and friends suggested that it was possible for him to continue his studies in the Dominican. With the blessing of his family he moved, only to find that Dominican universities were not readily accessible to Haitians. Undaunted, he sought out a tutor who would teach him the practical application of his knowledge and he began to look for employment. Shortly after his arrival in the Dominican he was introduced to Elio Madonia and began to learn business administration from him. Byrvens settled into the town of Ascension and immediately found an Italian craftsman to tutor him in the practical aspects of woodworking, while he worked in the woodworking shop building the doors and windows for the Samaritan Foundation projects. He has personalized a verse in the scriptures that he feels pertains to his life story.

"He (God) decided exactly when they should live. And He decided exactly where they should live." (New International Readers Version.) Acts 17:26

When the woodworking shop was moved to Paradise, Byrvens was resigned to the fact that he would stay in Ascension because he was Haitian and Paradise was a Dominican village. As he watched the village of Paradise grow he knew that it would be a very special place. "Then," his face lights up, "one day they called me to say that I should come and select the home that

my family would want to live in. My wife was so happy!"

Byrvens now runs the woodworking shop in Paradise Village. He builds and instructs others in constructing all the pews and pulpits for the churches, cabinets and furniture for the mission-aries, and all of the doors and windows for the houses that are being constructed.

But Byrvens also has a higher calling, a deeper purpose. "I have been given so many gifts," he says, "such as being raised in a loving, Christian home, an education, a free home, skills to make a living, and to help others. This is where my heart really lies, in helping others." He nods his head, clearly enjoying his thoughts. "The thing I like to do is talk to other people about God." The joy is evident on his face." I always have a group of people that I teach about God. I also like to teach them how to live in a village, a community, and how to get along."

"We are all living together. We are community," he says with pride.

The Faculty of Sewing & Tailoring

On a short stroll through Paradise Village we came upon a lady, fabric in hand and deep in thought. Clearly she was

determining how best to repurpose the drape she held. We went to chat with Christina Luñez. She showed us her spotless home and pointed out her certificates on the wall, indicating that she had completed two levels of sewing and tailoring and proudly showed us the sewing machine someone had given her as a gift. Cheerful curtains cover her windows and provide privacy to the bedroom and bathroom. Besides making her home a brighter place, she is now able to sew for others and bring in a small income. She has been hired to sew curtains for all the windows in the vocational school buildings.

Jim tells of one lady who simply sat despondent in her house day after day. When the sewing centre opened, she agreed to come, after much prodding. Now, seven months later, she is enthusiastic about the skills she has mastered and says, "Now I want to be out learning." An opportunity never before experienced has opened her mind to new possibilities.

The Faculty of Agriculture & Gardening

Scant years ago the fertile land in and around Villa Paradise lay untouched and unproductive. The board recognized this as a potential answer to the need for daily food that the villagers faced. It was an opportunity to help the people to help themselves. The idea of the gardens was born.

A large section of land was divided up into individual garden plots so that families could learn how to grow food to feed their families. Ed & Sylvia Rypstra from Ontario moved to the village for a year to set the program in motion. Greenvalley Equipment, the farm implements dealer from Manitoba, was eager to sponsor this venture because it was such a good fit with their interests. Infotep, the government adult education program, has chosen this site for their current focus of agricultural training on the northern coastline of the country.

Today, at the end of a long day's work, you will see families from the community walking together to their garden plots, filled with joy for the harvest that is producing an abundance of fresh fruits and vegetables to feed their families.

The Faculty of Adult Literacy

On the day that applications were being taken for the adult literacy classes, the lineup was quick in forming. They are only able to accommodate twenty-five students per intake, so many were turned away, but plans are underway to add portables and to increase the grade levels each year.

Isabel Martinez, a loving and gentle mother of three lively sons, calls me to her kitchen table. She is so thrilled to offer hospitality in the home that she shares with her husband, and smiles as

she sweeps aside the children's hair ornaments she is making. She brings me three notebooks and opens them proudly to show me her work. She has completed one level of adult literacy. It is clear that she is an intelligent woman. Each page is lined with red check marks indicating perfect work. When she has the money to pay for more notebooks her desire is to enroll in the second level. The cost is about fifty cents per book. But for now illness, parenting, and the need to feed

and clothe her family rob her of this luxury. We give her the few pesos and when we returned the next day she came running out of her house showing us her new notebooks.

While there is no current sponsor for this program, many donors contribute to its ongoing work through Jim and Debra's organization, Island Light Ministries.[18]

The Faculty of Hair Design & Barbering

The staff and administration at Spa Utopia and Salons and Utopia Academy in British Columbia, Canada, believe strongly in reaching out to their community and to their world. Some of the staff worked extra hours and holidays to contribute toward the sponsorship of the Barbering & Hair Design program.

Thirty-five year old Guillermo Compres sports a handsome haircut and trim beard, evidence of his participation in the barbering program. He has arisen as a natural leader in the community. His wife is a teacher in the elementary school. Prior to receiving a home in Paradise, they lived in the flood zone by the river because it was an area where they did not need to pay rent. When we ask him to share his story with us, he becomes almost lost in his memories and tears threaten to surface. He slowly nods his head and looks at

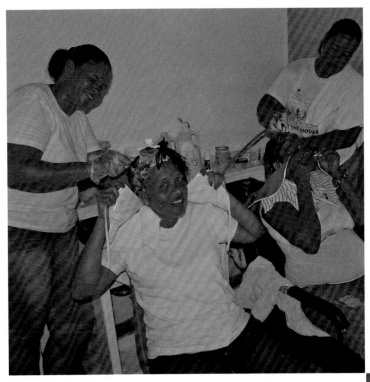
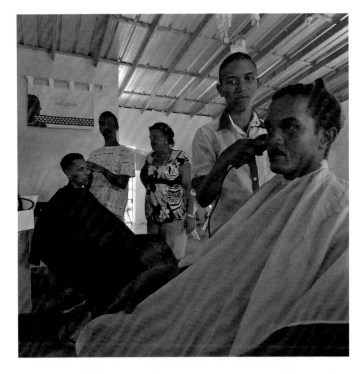
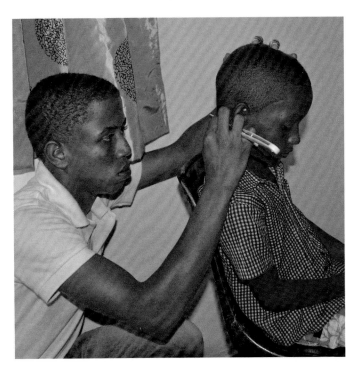

us, emotions still shimmering in his eyes. "It was difficult. Very difficult." He pauses. "I worked so hard all my life to provide for my family, and in two hours, you can lose everything." He raises his hand, fingers splayed. "Five times," he says. "Five times the river took everything. Everything! The last time I even had a fridge!" Sometimes he would get a call while he was at work and he would be told that the river was rising and his wife and children were in their house. He would race home wondering if he would get there in time. Each time his family was safe but everything was lost in the heartless torrent of the river.

During his growing up years Guillermo had been a follower of God but as he grew into young adulthood and got married he forgot his faith and filled his hours with women, alcohol, and drug abuse. "When we are young we think we are like Superman and we know everything but we are actually blind. Deceived." Now he knows that God has a special plan for him, for everyone.

I asked him how he felt when he received his home. His face lights up. He doesn't have enough exciting words to describe the change, but he knows that his life has changed at least ninety-five percent. "When I opened the door and walked into my house for the first time, I understood that this was the house that God had chosen for me. This was my home. I don't need a big house, a big yard, a pool in my back yard, or a fancy car." The moment that was most special

was the instant he understood that his wife and children would be safe. They would not have to live in fear any longer.

"God has a special plan for each one of us, but we need to persevere," he adds. When I ask him how it has affected him to be the recipient of this gift, he responds that he now spends more time in prayer, cares more deeply for people, and has more compassion. "I don't only pray for people in need, but also..." he points to each one of us and nods.

The Faculty of Electrical & Plumbing and Small Engine Repair

At the time of writing, these two faculties are in the start-up stage. While there are no consistent sponsors, ongoing startup costs are being provided by various groups and individuals.[19]

We look forward with anticipation to the opportunities this will provide to the adults in the village.

Community Life

If trees could tell stories, the big old shade tree near the entrance to the village would have many to tell. It was near the shade of this tree that Elio received the money to purchase the land for Paradise. It was under the shade of this tree that Elio and Ben dreamed of the possibilities of

a new village. It was under this tree that expectant faces waited to have their names called to receive keys to their new homes. Even after the village was complete the people seemed drawn to gather there, to visit, to catch the soft breezes that might grant them some reprieve from the heat of the day. It seemed appropriate that this gathering place should receive some special treatment.

Larry Neese, a landscaper from Florida, drafted a landscaping design for the area and donated all the plants to create a tropical paradise at the gathering place and around the public buildings. A team from Paradise Ranch in B. C. offered their blood, sweat, and I'm fairly certain their tears to transform the drawings into a lush,

tropical town centre, complete with a stone terrace, tables, and benches. Surrounded on one side by the senior housing complex and on another by the clinic, the gathering place offers the elderly a comfortable place to stay in touch with their community, and the sick a place to rest while waiting to get into the clinic. The municipal bus line has added one more bus stop to their route, right under the shade of that big old tree.

A village is only a small cluster of houses and buildings, but the people living in those houses make it a community. The residents of Paradise are definitely making their village a community.

In January of 2012, a grand celebration was held to commemorate the completion of Villa Paradise. Many of the donors attended and were

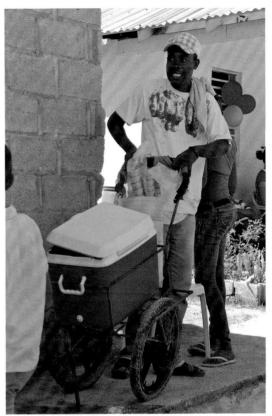

able to meet with the families whose lives had been impacted.

Chris Petkau went on the initial work trip with the Spruceland group in 2006 and helped to construct the school in Esperanza, among other projects. He and his wife, Gwen are busy parents of four, so while their hearts were drawn to the families in the Dominican they were busy raising their own and were unable to go again. This however, did not dampen their zeal. All their extra nickels, dimes, and dollars were gathered

up, and over a six-year period they were able to provide homes for twenty-three families. It was an emotional time when Chris and Gwen came for the celebration and were able to meet the families who now enjoy a safer present and a brighter future.

Chris and Gwen did not come to the Dominican alone, but brought with them Gwen's parents to share in the celebration with them. There are no chance encounters, no lost invitations in God's domain. Bill and Rosella Vanee's hearts were touched and overwhelmed as they

witnessed the hope, the transformation that their children's gifts had brought to these precious families. Stirred with compassion, they opened not only their hearts but also their purse strings to purchase homes for those in need. All of the houses in Paradise had already been sponsored and paid for but, very unexpectedly, a new village had been started just down the road. This donation would complete the financial requirements for homes for yet another village – Villa Zion. At the celebration for the completion of one village, the houses for the next village were already paid for. Another school was already in the making nearby.

Village #10 – Villa Zion

In 2006, because of an obvious need, Jaime Alonzo and his wife, Evely Peniche established a makeshift school in their open-air garage that would accommodate twelve students. The children had been coming for Sunday Bible classes and it was clear they could not read as they were not attending school. Evely started teaching them in the afternoons after coming home from her work as a teacher and psychologist in a local school. A family friend from Holland, Sacha Kok, worked alongside them.

The school grew to fill their whole home, and in January, 2010, the local government told Evely that she could no longer have a school there because of fire regulations. Thankfully, a two-story rental building nearby came available for the school and at this location they quickly grew to provide education for over two hundred children in classes up to grade seven. They had a staff of twelve part-time and full-time teachers. Jaime gave up his job at a local resort to help with school operations. They quickly outgrew even these accommodations and needed to expand.

Jaime and Evely contacted the Samaritan Foundation, asking if there was any possibility that there would be land and help available to build a new school. Years prior Elio had purchased a small plot of land that would suit their needs perfectly. Due to the urgent need, the board made a quick decision to assist them. Donations came in to cover the cost of construction for the Nest of Love School[20] and they were able to move into their new building for the 2011/12 season, only months later. About one hundred new children enrolled, bringing the total enrollment to almost four hundred. They are attempting to meet the demand by continuing to use the older rental property as well as this new building.

With the construction of the school on this parcel of land, and with a list of so many needy families, the Samaritan Foundation decided that they would build the seventy homes that this

plot of land could accommodate. So the village of Zion was established.

A group from the U. S. was cheerfully working in the heat of the day on the day we visited Zion. Another group from Canada worked at the lower end of the village. A team from England had just left for home. There are so many hundreds, and possibly thousands, of people that are a part of this on-going story. Each one has seen a need and played a part in changing the world with the gifts and strengths that they have been given.

Within months of the school opening, the homes were completed and a church was built. The pastor of the new church is himself a recipient of a new home and is now contributing to his community as their church leader.

The new citizens of Zion are transitioning peacefully into the rhythms of their new town with their new neighbours.

Vivacious Ana Julia Morarosa is waving us in to her home. She and her husband have been in the house for six months. He is at work. There is not a spot of dust to be seen in her home. When she opens the door, she instinctively grabs the broom and sweeps the doorstep. A well-read Bible is opened on the table.

This irrepressible woman cannot contain her joy at receiving a new home. We asked her how she felt when she knew she would receive a home. A huge smile lights up her face, she clasps her hands, and closes her eyes in a position of prayer. Then, unable to stay seated, she jumps up and dances around her chair. There are no words, but her gratitude is clearly evident. When she walked into her home that first day, she said, she just fell to her knees and stayed there all day, thanking God for this gift and the people who had provided it for her and her family.

On one of John and Ruth Unger's trips to Paradise, they joined a day trip that was going to visit the school in Zion, where they learned that many of the current students didn't have sponsors. They saw the quality of the educational program and wanted to help. Upon their return home they shared their hearts with their church community and invited them to join them in making a difference in the lives of the forgotten and downtrodden. Through this invitation, many, many children have been sponsored to attend school and several homes have been provided for. They have made several trips to the Dominican Republic since their initial visit, and each time they leave more of themselves in the Dominican and go home with more of the Dominican in their hearts.

The sign above Edobige Paylino's doorpost says, "I can do all things through Christ," and she lives by this motto every day of her life, literally trusting God for her strength as she nurses a bedridden husband. The father of her fourteen children abandoned her for other women, and

she took him in when he got sick and others abandoned him. He is paralyzed and has been under her care for many years. She cares for him because of the love of God in her heart, depending on Him for her daily food, patience, and grace. Many days she has no food for either of them, and it's obvious that medical supplies for his care are absent. She is an inspiring woman in her community.

Our interpreter, Stephanie, wanted very much to visit her friend, Jaime Jimenez, who had recently received a home. There is a raw quality still evident in the faces of the new residents; the strain and harshness of life has not yet been washed from their countenance. The past is still fresh in their present. Jaime and her husband lived near the river. He had a regular job but was severely injured in a motorcycle accident. The company paid for the initial surgery, but the leg was set incorrectly and he has great difficulty walking. Jaime was no longer able to work because she had to take care of her husband and their six children. They moved in with her mother, but soon after, her mother passed away and Jaime's brothers sold the home that had belonged to her. The family was now destitute. The Samaritan Foundation came to them and offered them a home. They are overwhelmed with thanksgiving. Two of their daughters are living with them. They cannot afford to feed six children, so with tears streaming down her face, Jaime tells us that whenever they can find enough money to go visit their other four children, they go to see them. I ask her how often this is. She hesitates and lifts her eyes to her husband's. The pain in their eyes is tangible. "A couple of times a year, maybe." They live less than an hour's drive away.

Stephanie leans down to talk to the school-age girls. "Do you attend the school?" she asks. They shyly nod their heads. "Why aren't you in school today?" she prods. "We can only go to school if we have eaten," is their response. "Were

you in school yesterday?" They drop their eyes and again shake their heads. The older daughter walks over to her mother and they simply hold each other. Stephanie turns her head, her heart aching for the people she loves so dearly. The family had not eaten for two days and there was no food in the house. But tonight they would eat.

Since then the Samaritan Foundation has implemented a daily nutrition program at the school as well as a weekly distribution of food to the families of the village.

I asked Jaime and her husband if they ever felt that God had forgotten them, if they ever lost hope. Immediately and indignantly they both cried, "No, never! He was our only hope, our daily strength. He has answered our prayers."

At times it seems that the pain of the world has become like blasé wallpaper through our constant exposure in the media, yet each face on the wallpaper represents a person with feelings and dreams for their loved ones.

Part Six
STRIDES TOWARDS SUSTAINABILITY

"Someone is sitting in the shade today because
someone planted a tree a long time ago."
-Warren Buffet

Village #11 – Villa Samaritano (Samaritan)

Development at Paradise was coming to a close. The houses in Zion were nearly complete and the leadership at the Samaritan Foundation thought they might just have a window of reprieve, a bit of a break. A novel thought, but it was not to be.

The leadership is perpetually looking for affordable land on which to build homes. Just as they were anticipating a lull of activity, a thirty-five acre property came available to them at a reasonable price, but it came with a couple of issues. It was landlocked; there was no way to access it. So they needed to purchase a small parcel of land from a neighbour to build an access road. A small waterway separated the two properties, so a bridge needed to be built. All this was possible, but they did not have the funds for it. Again, God intervened. Life Outreach International[25] from Texas agreed to partner with the Samaritan Foundation and provided the finances to buy the land.

The arduous task of town planning, surveying, registering, and applying for permits has begun and bureaucratic obstacles are being overcome

one at a time. The bridge to Villa Samaritano is now complete, and the Samaritan Foundation is hopeful that infrastructure and home construction will begin before the end of 2013.

Meanwhile work teams continue to come but progress on this project seems to be at a standstill. As we have witnessed throughout this account, when God closes a door, he always opens a window.

Villa Paradise #2

That window opened to them almost immediately when a plot of farmland came available directly across the street from Villa Paradise, adjacent to the vocational training centre, and directly across the street from the beautiful gardens. The land was acquired and initial construction has begun. Approximately one hundred more families will be able to enjoy the opportunities available to them in the village of Paradise. God had blessed the foundation with His divine assistance once again.

With projects layering one on top of another and multiple teams working in various locations, the administrative, leadership, and management responsibilities of the Samaritan Foundation escalated. Up until this point, they had been operating out of several home offices, but it was evident that they needed a central location to coordinate their efforts. Their new office building now welcomes all visitors at the entrance to Paradise 2, directly across the street from the Gardens of Paradise. The pressures of the growing load had been weighing heavily on John

and Jane Huizinga, and they had been praying for someone to help them. We have all heard the expression, "Leaders rise to the top." Well, this is exactly what is happening in the Dominican Republic.

Thirty-one-year-old Ermis Peniche is one of them. He carries an energetic positivity with him and greets me in perfect English. Intelligent eyes focus intently on me through his glasses. Two years ago he, his wife, and two daughters received a home in Paradise, and their lives have changed more than one could ever imagine.

Ermis grew up in extremely poor circumstances, the son of a pastor in the Dominican Republic. He put his faith in God at an early age and was able to finish high school, but much to his disappointment, university was out of their financial reach. He taught himself English as a child by sneaking into stores and bars, and visiting neighbour's homes where he could watch television. His favorite show was McIvor. He smiles at the recollection. "But I don't like TV now," he adds. "The new shows have nothing good in them."

Ermis had been working twelve to sixteen hour days as a supervisor in a food company for six years but was still only earning enough money for transportation. "I worked so hard, always doing my best, thinking I would get a raise." He had to walk two miles in the dark to catch the 5 a.m. bus to work and most of the year in the rain.

All this and he did not earn enough to even buy food and clothing for his family. It was destroying their marriage.

It was during an exceptionally rainy season that their marriage was at an all-time low. His love for his wife is clearly written on his face and the desperation of that season still carries pain in the telling. It was on one of the darkest, rainiest days that a glimmer of light finally broke through. At a ceremony under the protective branches of the big shade tree in the centre of Paradise, Ermis and his wife heard their names called and they received the keys for their new home. "My wife just cried and cried." The safe, dry, rent-free home came just in the nick of time, although they were still in dire need. He remembers crying out to God in desperation one morning, "God, I need to find work that will support my family! I have no money! We have no food in the house, and only a tiny bit of formula for the baby!" He had to walk to look for work, but the torrential rains that day made it impossible.

Sometimes the rain is a hindrance, but on this particular day it was a blessing. "It was only because it was raining so heavily that day that I met Pastor Jim. I watched him come towards the house. He had a gift for us from the people who sponsored our house. Sixteen hundred pesos! That was huge! I was able to feed my family and this could tide us over so I could find a better job." His heart was overwhelmed with gratitude

for this generous donor and he would so love to express his gratitude to him in person. "I believe his gifts not only saved our lives, but also our marriage."

Pastor Jim Tunnycliff was amazed at Ermis' fluid and easy grasp of the English language and began to recommend him for translation work for visiting teams that came to the Dominican Republic. He began to earn more in one week than he had in a whole month of work. The tide had turned. He was able to spend more time with his daughter and his wife. "I had to come up with some new techniques to win my wife back. That's very hard." He paused, remembering. "It takes a lot of time. It hurts a lot. But it's worth it!" His eyes twinkled. "We now have another daughter!"

One day Pastor Jim mentioned that John Huizinga, the Director for the Samaritan

Foundation, was looking for a person to be his right-hand man, someone he could trust. "Wow! I didn't know if I was that person. I didn't know if I could trust myself! I had a driver's license, but I didn't feel so confident that I could do what he wanted me to do." He was quiet for a moment and added, "He trusted me. It was a scary step, but I took it." He is now working in leadership alongside John, and has stepped very competently into the responsibilities that the job demands.

"Our lives have changed SO much in the last two years. Oh my, like, upside down! Life now? Oh! Happiness. So many blessings have happened in my life, so I can only be thankful. I received a home! And I received a job! And I got my wife back!"

"God is making me patient," he continued. "He's giving me knowledge and understanding to keep up with John. John is a great guy. He's my brother, a second father, and I admire him a lot. He trusts me and I trust him. We're partners. We're a team. We're friends."

As he speaks, I see that he has stepped into the role of leadership. "We have a lot of work to do and we need your help. We have a lot of projects that we would like to start." He has caught the vision. A leader has risen to the top.

Twenty-four-year-old Stephanie Delarosa is a strong, beautiful young lady with a confidence and grace beyond her years. She currently works as John Huizinga's assistant. Stephanie identifies with the young children she encounters, knowing their hunger and reading their fears because she once was one of them.

She recalls the pain of growing up in a home surrounded by constant fighting. Her mother was an alcoholic and her father a truck driver who had girlfriends in other cities, and even another family. He eventually moved in with his other family and her mother's drinking increased. What money she was able to earn went first to alcohol, even above food and rent. Stephanie remembers well the stress of trying to find excuses and pleading with their many landlords when the family received one eviction notice after another. It was a lot for a child to carry. Their greatest need was food for each day. Eventually a kind elderly German man moved in with them and their basic needs were taken care of for a short time, but he soon moved back to Germany, taking her mother with him. At the age of seventeen Stephanie was left to provide for her four siblings. Her older brother was a drug addict and, she shares, "This made life quite difficult. It is only by the grace of God that we are alive."

Throughout this time her father kept in touch and would give her money to go to school. She finished high school and he urged her to learn English, which she did. She prayed to God that she could find a job where she could perfect her English skills and convinced the owner of

particular restaurant because it was a place where they truly could escape from the work of the day. They were drawn to Stephanie and found out that they had a common bond in their faith. With the responsibilities of this rapidly growing ministry weighing them down, they had begun looking and praying for an assistant for John. When they offered Stephanie the position, she accepted and has been flourishing in her new role.

Today she walks confidently yet compassionately through the villages, comforting and encouraging those in pain, affectionately rubbing children's heads, always scanning life in the village around her as she does so. "When I visit the villages, I'm just so happy. I teach the people to respect their town, to be grateful for what they have been given. Excuse me," she says and walks over to a child who has just dropped a piece of paper on the ground. She taps him on the shoulder and speaks gently but firmly. The child runs over to the piece of garbage and tosses it in a nearby bin. He looks back at her for approval and she gives him a nod and a smile. She is often awed that the people treat her with such respect. "You have to be kind and you have

an English-speaking restaurant to give her a job. In fact, the owner spoke no Spanish whatsoever. She didn't earn a salary because he did not believe that women were as good as men; she could try to prove her worth and take home whatever tips she earned. So for twelve hours a day she literally ran back and forth serving customers while her male colleagues sauntered back and forth, earning their keep. Because she was a hard worker and so pleasant she was able to provide for the family from her tips.

Coincidentally, or perhaps providentially, it was John and Jane Huizinga's habit to go out for dinner each Friday night, and they chose this to be strong, and I believe it's my responsibility to teach them to understand that they have to take care of everything they have because it was a gift."

Her mother has since moved back to the Dominican Republic and has become a follower of Christ. She was instantaneously and immediately healed from her alcoholism. Today she and Stephanie's brother volunteer a lot of their time helping the poor alongside Stephanie.

Stephanie walks with the confidence of one who has found her place in life. "Now I know what I want to be. Now I know what God is calling me to be."

Other Jobs

To witness the emergence of hope, to watch it quickly blossom into dreams and action, is truly a spectacular experience. The single act of giving these people a hand up in the form of a home, infuses them with energy and vitality, and seems to fast forward some of them to step directly into their dreams. Perhaps existing in deprived and restricted conditions has helped narrow their focus in a way that we over-stimulated North Americans may not identify with.

"If only I had the opportunity, I would love to…" We've seen that almost immediately the entrepreneur opens a small shop in the front room, the artist begins to paint murals on his walls, the gardener finds flowers and vegetables to beautify her yard. Impromptu barbershops are open for business on front patios. Individuals begin to market their talents. All they need is someone to see their plight and offer them a hand up, a platform from which to grow on their way to independence and self-sufficiency.

With each new village that is built, a new economic infrastructure is created that presents new opportunities for employment. New schools provide job opportunities for teachers and support staff. The freedom that comes from not having to pay rent has allowed many to buy bicycles or motorcycles that assist them in bringing in an income.

A local man has been hired as the building supervisor for all the projects of the Samaritan Foundation and many local men are employed in the construction process.

One home in Paradise features a barber chair sitting on its front steps. Oscar Reyes Martinez radiates happiness. His friend taught him to be a barber and he has many clients. He has earned enough money to add some architectural details to create an attractive front porch. His wife has become a teacher at the local school. When he is asked what the biggest change in his life is, his smile grows. "The biggest change is that I am a Christian now. That is the biggest change." Sometimes in the hustle and bustle of life, when things are going well, we neglect the cry of our

soul. Oscar and his wife recognized where true happiness, true fulfillment, comes from.

But self-sufficiency does not happen as quickly for some as for others. Many need to first learn skills, many need employment, and many are ill from years of poor diet, contaminated drinking water and lack of medical care. Some are simply too old to be able to work.

While great energy has been and continues to be spent on the development of villages and educational, spiritual and medical growth, the fact remains that unemployment or underemployment is a hurdle that often takes some time to overcome. Humanitarian organizations find themselves at a delicate juncture much like that of being a parent. How can we equip them for the future? How can we encourage independence and at the same time take care of their vital needs for today?

Food Distribution

It became apparent early on that some families simply were not able to eat every day. In response to this the Samaritan Foundation began a weekly food distribution program to outlying villages, which they supplement with milk for infants and toddlers.

In addition, the schools have been able to institute nutrition programs in all of the Samaritan Foundation villages. Josie and Kim

Pensinger of Dominican Advance run the schools in both Nazareth and Paradise. They are passionate about the feeding program and have witnessed evidence of its necessity.

While it is not the intention of the Samaritan Foundation to build dependence on food handouts, the harsh reality is that some families living in these villages still go without food on a regular basis. Neighbours and friends look out for each other and help as they can. There is still a long way to go in job creation and laying the groundwork for sustainable employment opportunities.

Apart from this, a food distribution centre has been built in the village of Paradise, which provides jobs for some and volunteer opportunities for many. Stephanie Delarosa not only works as John's assistant, she also oversees the work and distribution of this operation.

The Gleaners Ontario[21] provides humanitarian organizations with barrels of dehydrated soup at no cost to the recipients. They receive excess or non-marketable produce from farmers, produce packing plants, and distribution centres. It is trimmed, diced, dehydrated, and packaged into three-pound soup packages containing one hundred servings of soup each. This volunteer driven Canadian organization began operations in 2008 and by 2012 had shipped 7.1 million servings of soup to thirty countries around the world. One of these countries is the Dominican Republic and the distribution centre is in the village of

Paradise. Here volunteers and workers add rice and spices to the dehydrated vegetables to make a complete meal for an entire family. Food preparation instructions are given to the families when they are distributed. Rice is used instead of beans because it cooks more quickly. The cost of firewood and the long cooking time required for beans makes it unaffordable for them.

Medical Strides

In some respects the stride of change in the countryside of the Dominican Republic is fast-paced and steady, yet there is still a huge chasm to cross before the gap between the rich and the poor narrows, before medical aid and the necessities of life are accessible to all.

Board member Tore Stautland has been working diligently in the medical arena as an advocate for the poor. Dr. Bob Ameligmeyer and Sister Teodora have tirelessly taken care of the many medical needs at the only public hospital in Puerto Plata that serves about 400,000 people.

Although the building was condemned after an earthquake in 2004, no plans have been made to replace the facility and so they do the best they can with what they have. We visited the hospital in 2006 and were appalled. There were only two wards, the maternity ward and all others. Visitors were allowed to wander in and out at will and take any and all photos they wished.

We were among the visitors one day. In the hallway a young boy played with a lizard using a thread as a leash. We stepped into the first room. Twenty beds lined the lengths of the room. Chained to the first bed was a prisoner with gunshot wounds in his side and leg. Across from him was a little boy with dengue fever, his

mother holding him helplessly. Feverish, often bloody and sweaty bodies lay on green rubber mattresses with no sheets or pillows for comfort or protection. The stench of infection and illness lay heavy in the air, as tangible as the despair and hopelessness in the eyes that turned towards us. The vented concrete blocks near the ceiling did nothing to move the stagnant air in the room. Where was that familiar smell of disinfectant that greets us in our North American hospitals? A few relatives came in with food for their loved ones. The hospital budget allows for little more than a slice of bread and some thin porridge. A hallway with doors to rooms just like this one stretched before us. We were introduced to Dr. Bob as he was making his rounds. He gives his life to serve the sick and the dying in the Dominican Republic.

We stepped next door into the closet that was the cleaning station, a small area perhaps six feet by six feet. The area above, around, and below the single sink was rusted and stained. Old dirty plastic bleach or vinegar containers with the tops cut off were strewn about. Not a drop or bottle of disinfectant could be seen. Their funds for those luxuries had been depleted for the last several months. I imagined the man with the open bullet wounds being chained to a sweaty, germ infected rubber mattress. Who had lain there before him? Was it someone infected with AIDS or dengue fever? What of the frail old woman, hardly visible beneath the shriveled skin

sagging over her worn out and weary bones? How could she overcome her own maladies while fighting off the possible infection of the previous patient? The whimper of children brought me back to the present and we moved on to the maternity ward.

What joyful places, maternity wards! New mothers raised glowing faces towards us as they cuddled their precious bundles, so fresh from heaven, and nurtured them close to their breasts. Yet, interspersed with the joyful were tormented faces, weeping, gazing with empty arms at the newborn babies in nearby beds. All mothers recuperated in the same room, those whose babies lived and those whose babies did not. Thankfully this practice has changed since 2006 through the work of Tore, Dr. Bob, Sister Teodora, and others.

We entered the room where blood transfusions were administered. Eight people sat in reclining chairs about the room. Two small fridges held the available blood but, the nurse explained, one of the fridges had not been working for the last two years. The four or five bags of blood supply visible through the glass door of the working fridge would not be enough for the eight people in the room. They would need to wait until someone brought some from Santo Domingo, but it was a long and hot trip and so they were not sure when that would be. The nurses shrugged their shoulders helplessly.

A heart to help does not always mean that you are able to do so.

One couple in our group took Dr. Bob aside and asked what was wrong with the defeated looking young man lying on one of the blue mattresses. He looked to be in his early 20s, about the age of their two sons. "He needs a blood transfusion," was the reply. "What would it cost," they asked, "to send someone to Santo Domingo to get blood and bring it for this young man?" "Less than a hundred American dollars," was the surprising response. The gentleman took a hundred dollar bill from his pocket and asked Dr. Bob to please see that the trip was made and that this young man would get the blood he needed. The remaining dollars would buy him some food.

The needs were overwhelming in that place and yet, as in all places of illness or desperation, when we stop to see the needs and look at what might be in our hand to give or to do, we see that we can make a huge difference. We can completely change the course of so many lives. We can change the world, one person at a time.

We were led to the dispensary and our first introduction to Sister Teodora. She is affectionately but reverently called 'The Sergeant'. All of the medications that Tore ships to the Dominican Republic are received, tabulated, and distributed by Sister Teodora and the other sisters in the nearby convent. "Sister Teodora has been our strongest ally in the DR," he says. "She receives the medical containers and distributes the meds and supplies to over eighty clinics and ten hospitals across the island. We could not have achieved what we have without her."

She stands strong yet soft behind the wicket, taking each prescription from the line of patients as they come to her window. There is a certain kindness in her no-nonsense mannerism. Each tablet, each vial, is carefully noted in her distribution records. There is no room for error and she is quick to notice if someone tries to sneak back into line for a second turn.

By law all medical doctors must donate a few hours of their time to the public hospital each week, so several come from 7:00 till 9:00 in the morning. They will see as many patients as they can, diagnose and prescribe, but when the clock strikes 9:00 they leave for their private clinics and paying customers. The patients come to Sister Teodora, hopeful that she might have the required medication free of charge. If she doesn't they turn away, worry and despair drooping their shoulders. In so many cases poverty has made them wait too long to come to the hospital in the first place and poverty holds the necessary medication out of reach. They turn away, perhaps to stand in line again tomorrow for another prescription, perhaps to return to their homes to await the unknown.

Part Seven

HOPE FOR TOMORROW

"The future depends on what you do today."
-Mahatma Ghandi

Hope for the Future

The Minister of Health has presented the Samaritan Foundation with the unique opportunity of making a capital investment towards a new general hospital in Puerto Plata. Despite the fact that visiting groups and individuals have invested time and equipment towards improving the current condemned facility, like most public health facilities in the country, it is still operating at subpar standards. In spite of its condemned status, the government has spent very little on improvements, and as a result it lacks some of the most basic services. "Due to significant shortages," Tore Stautland says, "we have sent several containers of medicine and medical supplies over the last few years. Sanitation disciplines are disappointingly in short supply. No disinfection protocols are in place, which leads to the spread of infection and other unnecessary health risks. Public hospitals and health care facilities have deplorable sanitation records, and recently health officials had to investigate the deaths of sixteen newborns in the capital's largest maternity hospital, hinting that unhygienic conditions were to blame. Unless families take the role of primary caregiver the patient will receive little to no care. Doctors continue to diagnose and write prescriptions but the patients are often unable to pay for the prescription required for recovery. Furthermore, we have found little to no pediatric care so patients have to travel for over an hour to the closest pediatric health care facility, which is prohibitive for the average person living in poverty."

Tore goes on to say that through a relationship with the Minister of Health, many improvements have been made, but there is still evidence of urgent need. In addition to inadequacies in prenatal, delivery, and peri-natal care, critical preventative education and training must be implemented to begin an assault on the rampant spread of such diseases as tuberculosis, HIV/ AIDS, and sexually transmitted diseases. The distribution of basic needs such as de-worming medicines, vitamins, and oral hygiene kits would go a long way in addressing common, unnecessary illnesses. Because of inaccessibility, rural Dominicans suffer from an even higher rate of disease. The challenges in the Dominican Republic are great.

A Children's Hospital

It was Sister Teodora who encouraged Tore to consider the idea of building a pediatric hospital, and they decided to look into the possibilities. "As this project was going to be significantly more complex than building schools, medical clinics, and houses, we needed to find centrally located land, hospital equipment, and a tailored agreement with the government to proceed," Tore explained.

"The vision has grown into a plan, which is to build and operate a state of the art forty-bed hospital with a fully functional operating theatre, along with educational facilities, thereby vesting new paradigms, disciplines, and standards into an otherwise archaic medical system. By radically changing the health services culture in the DR, and aggressively administering services and medication at a preventative level, an opportunity exists for the first time to actually manage and ultimately eradicate numerous diseases and persistent, even deadly contagions that today are seriously afflicting thousands of DR's population.

The closest pediatric hospital is in Santo Domingo and most parents can't afford to go there. It is heartbreaking to see children die unnecessarily because they don't have funds to go to a private clinic. Furthermore, the Haitian children are systematically ill-treated and given significantly reduced service and overall care. The government is trying to introduce medical cards to Dominicans, which will prevent any 'illegal' resident from receiving any care at all. While I understand this problem of economics," Tore continues, "my desire is to build a structure at no cost to the government with the caveat that they have to have a 'no child turned away' policy. The opportunity to participate in the development of this desperately needed hospital facility, and the resources that have already been committed, is staggering by any measure."

Miraculously, through a mutual contact, a 15,000 square meter piece of prime property was donated. "We could not have asked for a better location for the hospital," Tore exclaims. "It is centrally located and accessible to the whole region. All local bus services stop a few hundred feet from the property."

Peacock and Lewis, a large architectural firm out of Florida, has a long history in designing sophisticated medical facilities. They have finished all the drawings and the blue prints are complete. Additional thought has been given to environmental dangers such as earthquakes, hurricanes, tropical heat and humidity. Tore's largest supplier of medicine and hospital supplies has officially offered to supply all the medical equipment required including an X-ray machine, anesthesia machine, heart monitors, and a dialysis machine. "The value of this is close to six million dollars, so we are quite excited. A portion of the money required for the building itself has been committed, but not its entirety. The government has granted a verbal agreement to operate and staff the hospital at their cost, but a written agreement is proving to be very difficult to attain." Tore concludes, "Though the need is indeed overwhelming, the opportunity is now

ours to make a huge difference in the healing of one life at a time."

High School

While plans for medical advancement are moving along, other developmental programs are also moving forward.

In the village of Paradise, Dr. Kim and Josie Pensinger of Dominican Advance continue to persevere in improving access to quality education that will prepare impoverished young Dominicans to enter universities and other schools of learning. The need for an accessible high school for the students in their K-8 schools is paramount. There is only one public high school in Sosua and the daily bus or taxi fare makes it cost prohibitive for those in outlying areas to attend. "We are getting these children into our schools and teaching them to dream. We are telling them that they can be doctors, lawyers, nurses, or anything they would like to be, and they begin to aspire. But then, when they get to grade eight, it becomes impossible for them to go on to high school to get the education that is required to fulfill their aspirations. It is almost worse to teach them to dream and then to snatch it from them than not to teach them to dream at all," says Kim Pensinger.

They went on the search for available land in the area and purchased a small parcel with the limited funds that they had. The land is near Paradise and is easily accessible from all surrounding villages. They proceeded to draw up plans for a technical, accredited university entrance high school with computer labs, a place that would provide students a smooth transition into university. With the villages popping up so quickly all around Paradise, it became evident almost immediately that the planned facility would not be large enough to provide high school education for the six hundred families in the vicinity, and yet, it was all they had.

When Onofrio Miccolis received an invitation to the groundbreaking ceremonies for the new high school, which were to take place the following day, he went to take a look.

When he saw the limitations of the property, he called fellow board member, Ben Sawatzky and they started talking about the need for a larger high school and for more land. They wanted to help, so they began to inquire about available property, and as providence would have it, they found an adjacent parcel available at a reasonable price. Rev. Miccolis and Ben engaged in a 24-hour awareness and fund-raising campaign. Their desire was to raise the full amount required for the adjacent property prior to the groundbreaking ceremonies, so that this exciting news could be included in the grand announcement at the celebration. This gave them less than twenty-four hours. The Ben Sawatzky

Foundation, the Samaritan Foundation, and Christian Life Relief International,[22] under the leadership of Rev. Miccolis, pledged the funds that totaled half the amount required to purchase the additional 3200 square metres. Hours before the groundbreaking ceremonies were to begin, Ben received an email from young businessman, Adam Dirksen of Innova Homes in Stony Plain, Alberta[23]. He just emailed to say that he had funds available that he would like to donate towards the Dominican Project. It was exactly, to the dollar, what they needed to complete the purchase! Adam has never visited the Dominican but he has sponsored the building of thirteen homes. He had no knowledge of the school project or the need for that exact amount of money, nor of the ceremonies that would happen within hours of his pledge.

Onofrio Miccolis received the news when he was already seated, waiting for the function to begin. He was able to surprise the Pensingers and all those in attendance with this exciting news. "There was not a dry eye in the gathering," Onofrio shared.

So the Pensingers are back at the drawing board with the architects, designing a larger school, dreaming of the future these children can have with a quality high school education. While the funds are not in yet to complete the building, history has taught us to be confident in God's provision.

Part Eight
MAKING A DIFFERENCE

"If not us, then who? If not now, then when?
– John Lewis

There is a deep and certain joy that comes in offering someone a hand up, in sharing what you have to help someone in need. Elio himself was the recipient of a hand up. Three American women sponsored his immigration from Italy to Canada back in 1950. Within a couple of years he had saved up enough money to pay them back but they refused his money. They told him that they had given a gift, not a loan, but he could use that money to help someone else. "As a result, I have been paying them back all my life." He pauses for a moment. "And it still feels good."

We spoke with some of the volunteers that were working there during our last visit, and each one of them would heartily agree with Elio. It feels good.

Faces of Volunteers

"**I** had something good happen to me and I want to pay it forward," says volunteer Darren Ferguson. "It's an eye opener to see how we can make such a difference."

Tom Stanford and his wife Shawna have come numerous times and have found that their whole life has been influenced and enriched.

They make friends with the villagers. Relationship is important to them. Tom says, "It's so much more than putting on roofs. We do what we can and in turn find we are more patient, more understanding of the faults of people around us. It puts the urgency and chaos in everyone's life at home into perspective." They even brought their children along one year to show them a different perspective on life. "I keep returning because it keeps life real," Tom shares.

Frieda Neufeld's life has been radically changed by volunteering. "The first time I came I realized the incredible opportunity to make a difference here. God planted a seed in my heart. I don't ever want to stop giving," she says passionately. She has come four times with plans to come again. "It has changed my life and my heart on a day-to-day basis. I see flashbacks of the DR regularly. Even when I feel I can't afford to go and yet commit to it, God provides the way. I never want to stop," she repeats again.

Eva Neufeld and her daughter came with Frieda. Eva is excited about her first trip. She says she walked through an open door. She loves to sew. Her excitement grew when she got to the Dominican and realized there was an unexpected opportunity to help in a sewing class at the vocational training centre. God had put what she felt was an ordinary talent to extraordinary use and gave her great fulfillment in the process.

Don Moen says, "These families took a piece of my heart and just filled it up. I want to keep doing this." At a time in Don's life when he didn't own his own home, he took a second job after hours to earn money to buy homes for the homeless in the DR. "I had to do something," he says, "and I'm happy inside. Everyone can do something!"

Ruben Sawatzky went on a work trip in 2006. While he has not returned for a second time, the impact of that single trip was tremendous. He and his wife Martha purchased a home for single mom, Aris Martinez Vasquez. It was a dreary, rainy day that we drove the van to pick up Aris from the shack she lived in with her two children, her mother, her sister, and her sister's children. When she emerged from the door, we saw the reason for the mission director's decision to give her a ride that day, while the other recipients walked. She was fully nine months pregnant, and had a one-and-a-half-year-old in one arm. She held her three-year-old son's hand as she slid down the slippery clay embankment to join us. Her husband had abandoned her two months prior. We placed her in the front passenger seat. I had a beautiful reflection of her face in the rear view mirror. She sat with a tiny smile, eyes alive with the joy of anticipation, head held high. It was evident that she felt like a princess, perhaps for the first time in her life.

I have observed the changes in Aris through the intervening years. She entered the village completely illiterate and emotionally devastated and depleted. A year later we visited the village and found Aris on her front step, working through her son's elementary math workbook, so excited with this new opportunity. Now, seven years later, she has completed her first level of adult literacy and her son is an outstanding student in the school. Her reticence has been replaced with joyful confidence. She doesn't like to think of the days prior to Paradise because it still brings on the darkness, but she finds great delight in encouraging others to keep hoping.

Upon Ruben's return, he shared his story with his brother-in-law, Marty Scheutz, and encouraged him to go. He did.

Marty has been to the Dominican seven times, twice with his wife and family. When their eight-year old daughter CJ saw the way other children her age were living, she knew she had to do something about it. When she got home, she created picture calendars from the photos they had taken there and sold these to her neighbours, her friends, and the people at their church. She sold enough to raise money for homes for two families. The following year this young aspiring artist sold her art collection and raised money for yet another home. Her two younger brothers caught the vision. They began to do odd jobs, extra chores, and anything they could find to earn a few dollars here, and a few dollars there, and each of them has also sponsored a home.

Marty challenged the church youth group to sponsor a home and they collected enough pop bottles to do just that in one day. That group, though never having visited the Dominican Republic, knows that the family in house #133 in Paradise has a home due to their efforts. Marty says it's all about timing. God nudges. A door opens. He was available so he walked through the open door. He enjoys sharing the opportunity and watching people respond. What a legacy he is leaving for his family, the youth group, and those who stop to listen.

Lorel Giesbrecht and her sister-in-law Christa went to teach a supplementary sewing class in the village of Paradise. They were touched by the realization that their job meant a lot more than just teaching skills, it was about building relationship with the women. It was a very pleasant and unexpected surprise, considering the language and cultural barriers. Lorel says, "I was able to see that these people in another culture and in another economic bracket have the same heart that I do in terms of loving their families, their children, their friends, and wanting to provide for them. They want to be prepared for the future. They want to be physically healthy and also to have healthy relationships with God and others. They want the same things for their family that I want for mine." The heart of a woman is universal.

84

Rae-Lynn Sprowl and her husband, Brian Moore, have gone to the Dominican Republic several times and have brought their young son with them. They are modeling to the next generation the impact of what a generous heart and hand can make.

Bethany, Katie, and Alli were three university students in Canada who heard the story of the Samaritan Foundation projects. They immediately wanted to help, but being students on a limited income they had no financial resources, so they looked at what was in their hands to give. They would plan an art auction. As art and music students, they had many contacts to draw upon. That first event brought in enough for them to sponsor a home. The next year they enthusiastically repeated their effort and raised money for garden plots for the homeowners. How excited they were. Though they are no longer in the university, their uncle, who teaches there, recently led a team of students to work on the project and to see firsthand the difference that the students' efforts have made. Moved by deep compassion, these girls used what was in their hands creatively to ease the burden of hurting families and drew others to join them.

For the past fifteen years Giuseppe, an Italian German, has been a rich asset to the volunteer community of Samaritan Foundation. He has sacrificed his golden years to help the poor.

"Thanks be to God because now I understand that life has meaning."

Ernie and Lella Properzi's hearts were captured by the people of the Dominican Republic on their very first visit. For years, their vacations had centred around long visits to their homeland, Italy. But now, they make frequent visits to the Dominican Republic, lovingly pouring into the lives of families where they see a need.

The following short story reflects the generous hearts of Willy and Irmgard Sawatzky, partners in Spruceland Millworks.

> A wise woman who was traveling in the mountains found a precious stone in a stream. The next day she met another traveler who was hungry and the wise woman opened her bag to share her food. The hungry traveler saw the precious stone and asked the woman to give it to him. She did so without hesitation. The traveler left, rejoicing in his good fortune. He knew the stone was worth enough to give him security for a lifetime. But a few days later he came back to return the stone to the wise woman.

"I've been thinking," he said. "I know how valuable the stone is but I give it back in the hope that you can give me something even more precious. Give me what you have within you that enabled you to give me the stone."

-Author unknown

A generous desire to share what is in one's hand is truly a great treasure of the human heart that reaps blessing in return.

There have been so many people involved in this project over the last twenty-four years that are not recognized in this book, but who have all played a vital role in this story of transformation. People that we have met, and people that we have not met are all represented by the legacy they have left in the Dominican Republic. Each one is important in God's plan. We are all cogs in a wheel, and when one cog is missing, the wheel's progress is stunted or comes to a standstill.

Many of those who give of their dimes and their dollars, their time or their talent, never have the opportunity to witness the impact of their giving. Some have the opportunity to come and readily engage with the family in the home they sponsored. Others stand back with quiet satisfaction and just watch the joy of changed lives. But no matter if one comes or gives, or does both, the impact of that generosity forever changes the hearts and lives of those who receive, and at the same time, it enriches and changes the heart of the giver.

Part Nine

THE JOY OF HOPE

"God has blessed me with His divine assistance."
– Onofrio Miccolis

Carmen Julia Rosario has been transplanted from a dark and hopeless reality. She is a single mother with five children. There was not even a small space in her heart for a glimmer of hope to shine through. She was resigned to the fact that her children would also be illiterate, poor, and trapped. When she received her home, she was so very happy. Although she doesn't have the money to attend the adult education programs, she has learned to read and write from the children's workbooks and through her study of the Bible. She has learned how to grow a garden to feed her family. Her sunny back yard is filled with fruit and vegetable plants and in the corner of the yard chickens cluck contentedly.

Carlos Quinones and Marielenos Acosta

"Our lives have changed 1000 x 1000! We have no words for the gratitude in our hearts." He tells us that he has been able to start a small business selling fish and as a result has been able to purchase a motorcycle to use as a taxi. This is life changing. "I try to be like a father in the community and help people when they can't agree." His influence is felt in the village.

Milvio Florentino and Clarivel Reyes

"Moving here was like going to heaven!" Milvio raises his hands towards heaven and says, "I had faith, big faith that God would help us." He is blind and tells us that his wife has gone for the day taking the children to a special school. They have cataracts and are nearly blind as he is. Milivio is thrilled that his children will now have the benefit of an education because of the

generous heart of a sponsor. He has a strong desire to contribute to their new community by helping others, sharing his faith, and even his food when he is able. This is a family being transformed.

Elminia Almontez Rosario, nicknamed China, is a radiant, gentle spirited single mom with three daughters. The location of her house gives her a uniquely large yard, and she has created a bountiful garden, surrounded by a fence that she has built. A wide rock sidewalk lined with flowers leads to her home. Though her journey as a single mom was not without desperate struggle, she now radiates a peace and a joy that she attributes to her faith. Prayer is a rich part of her life. She quietly pays attention to God's whisper in her soul, and reaches out to help others. She has found part-time employment as a housekeeper.

Lirio Almontez heard of the availability of homes through his cousin China. His situation was desperate. He came from a particularly dangerous area near the river, where he lived in a home owned by his in-laws. When his wife died of AIDS, they threw him out and he and his three young sons were destitute. Tears of gratitude well up as he explains that he never could have provided this kind of a home for his boys. It is a gift from God, and his heart has been changed as a result. To be just down the street from his cousin China is also a miracle. They can look out for one another. Again Lirio fights back tears as he shares his need to find employment to buy food for his family. He is so grateful for the school for his boys, and for the recently received garden plot. His appreciation for the church fellowship is evident; the comfort that it provides is like soothing ointment to an aching soul.

Maria Isabel Deleon proudly holds daughter Eugenia Maria Garsia, the very first baby to be born in the village of Paradise. She was born in their very own home. Her husband now has a motor taxi and so can travel to work in the city. Gratitude exudes from her, and she is convinced God has a special plan. Her prayers are filled with a confident hope for the future. A new generation has come into a brand new beginning. What hope!

Jose Agustin Abreo Polanco and Arabery DelaCruz Romero say, "Our lives have changed from hell to heaven." Both he and his wife are employed. She is away today working in the soup distribution centre. Jose is in charge of overseeing the garden plots. They are thrilled to be able to feed their four children. In return for their blessings they are committed to helping others, sharing their food with their elderly neighbours, and seeking to be an example. "We are content." That says it all.

Jakelin Sanche tells the familiar story of having to run in the night from the raging river. Her dad had applied for a home through the Samaritan Foundation but when he died, Jakelin took up the application. She was so excited to get this home. She had never imagined she would have this opportunity and cried when she realized it was true. She knew it was a gift from God. Jakelin's heart is not without its grief. She lost her two-year-old child here when she turned her back but for a moment. Time has passed since her initial anger toward God and those relentless 'why' questions. She still finds herself working her way back to trusting God. Working in her garden is good therapy, and it keeps her occupied while providing for her family. She tells us that she is now helping another Mom through a similar season of grief, and it is helping her at the same time.

She is learning that ultimately, she must make a choice when life is hard. She can choose to run with her anger into bitterness, or she can run into God to receive the comfort and strength she needs to carry her through.

Lorena Noel is a single mom with five children. She moved across the street from the desperate village of Algodones to the new village of Esperanza and no longer fears break-ins in the middle of the night because she has a secure door to her new home. From a one room hovel to a home with a kitchen, a bathroom, and a bedroom…. and water! It is so unbelievable to her, she exclaims, "My whole life has changed!"

Her joy is evident. As we talk together her mother, Lofita, arrives. She is sick, looking nine months pregnant with fluid on her stomach. "Our faith has grown so much," Lorena declares. "Now we are fasting and praying for my mother." The true definition of hope is, "confident expectation in God." Lorena truly has hope!

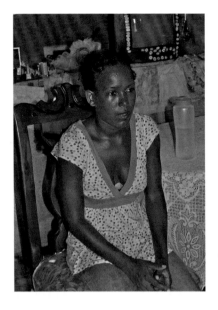

San Soir Desantil is busy at his morning task, filling water pails at the town tap for those who come for water. He takes it upon himself to see that this precious gift of clean water is not wasted. Taking my pen and paper, he proudly writes out his own name, and then, when we arrive at his home, he points to his plumbing certificate displayed on the wall. At this point, he is unable to afford transportation to go to the city where he might find employment in his trade, so he each day he contributes to community life in any way he can. "Every day," Sain Soir tells us, "I make a goal to achieve something." He volunteers in the town at the water tap; he serves on the town council; "I have a vision," he says. "God has changed our village and He will change our

community. I look for ways to change myself and help others." This man truly has been given new pride and value.

Mateo Luis welcomes us into his sparsely furnished home. As the self-declared Mayor of Esperanza he has a big heart to help the people of his village and makes himself available to them. His wife died eight years ago and life was very hard in the village of Los Algodones. "Very bad," he exclaims, shaking his head. When he moved to his new home in Esperanza two years ago, he gave most of his belongings, especially the kitchen things, to his sister down the street, who cooks for him and does his laundry. He is very happy to have a clinic nearby. He loves to go to church and says his heart is "mucho, mucho full, thanks be to God". Our visit is cut short when someone comes to get his help and he waves goodbye as he simply states he is needed. Yes, he is needed. Therein lies his fulfillment.

Our hearts are full as we leave the villages with our cameras and notebooks. We know things are not perfect here. We know not all stories are success stories. Many still have no

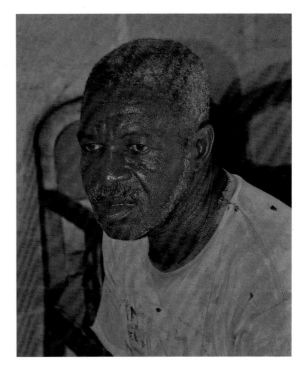

work, no faith, or even food, and problems exist as they do anywhere people live in community. Yet what we have experienced has changed our hearts: the profound gratitude, the contentment, the joy, the desire we saw over and over, to reach out and help another. Yes, we were made to be in community. We were made to touch another's life.

We leave blessed, inspired, and with a deep desire to do more, as we can, where we can. Though we came to build homes, we see that we have stepped into a story of building hope.

The wheels of change continue to turn in the Dominican Republic. Just as the landscape of the country is being transformed, so are the hearts and lives of the poor. Change has not only come to those living in poverty, but also to each one that has stepped out in response to the impulse of God in their hearts.

Much has been accomplished and much more is yet to be done as each individual faced with the need answers the question, "What are you going to do about it?"

"A simple vacation has become a great mission."
-Elio Madonia

Part Ten

A NOTE FROM GAIL

"You are unique in what you have to offer to the world."

– Gail Rodgers[24]

Making It Personal 1

It has been my incredible privilege to walk alongside Dori on this life changing journey of transformation. I am forever indebted for the invitation to join her ring-side seat in what God is doing in the Dominican Republic and elsewhere.

Throughout this story there are two themes that continually pop out to me. One is the invitation that one person extends to another, and the whole venture keeps blossoming as God connects the dots of lives and talents and resources. The second theme is the "yes" that willing people offer when an invitation is extended. The "yes" may seem like a "big yes" or it may appear a "small yes". This story offers examples of both. Yet in God's eyes every "yes" is important, every story an opportunity to invite others to join you. God blesses the yeses.

As we have interviewed, researched, and visited the site of this fascinating on-going story of hope, Dori and I have found our own hearts freshly challenged. We realized again that every day we have an opportunity to open our eyes afresh to the needs around us and to listen to the quiet whisper in our souls inviting us to step out and meet that need. Indeed they are invitations to a new page in our own stories.

Sometimes the busyness of our lives and agendas gets in the way of this most fulfilling adventure of reaching out. It may be across the world, or it may be across the room.

You may be a seasoned humanitarian with many pages in your own story to tell. Or you may find yourself new to this idea of looking and listening. Either way we invite you to respond to the invitation to write a fresh page, or a new chapter in your own story.

Therein lies true adventure!

Making It Personal 2

The story is told of a young boy walking the beach one morning tossing starfish back into the water from the dry beach where they had been swept by the waves. An old man approached him, laughingly telling him there were far too many washed up starfish to even think of making a difference throwing any back.

With a thoughtful look the boy picked up another starfish and, tossing it into the waves said, "It makes a difference to that one."

"If you can't feed a hundred people, then just feed one."
– Mother Teresa

Ordinary people DO make a difference when they walk with their eyes open.
- Open the eyes of your heart and see the needs right where you walk.
- Open the door of your heart and say "yes" to reaching out in some way.

Choose to be one who makes a difference.
Choose to look.
Choose to say 'yes'.

Therein lies true joy!

Making It Personal 3

What pulls for your attention?
- Is it children in distress?
- Is it the hungry? The homeless?
- The lonely? Those in pain?
- Is it education for the underprivileged?
- Those hurting emotionally and spiritually?

The needs around us can be overwhelming when we stop to actually look with eyes that see. We cannot meet them all. Pay attention to the needs that touch your heart. Learn the art of listening to your own heart.

You are unique in what you have to offer to the world.

Your talents, your experience, your way of doing things are needed by someone, somewhere. Open the ears of your heart and listen. Pay attention to what pulls at your heartstrings. God's quiet whisper in your soul is a call worth answering. Even today, listen with your heart.

"For we are God's workmanship, created in Christ Jesus to do good works, which God prepared in advance for us to do."
– Ephesians 2:10

Therein lies true purpose!

Making It Personal 4

Look at what is in your hand.
What can you share?
What can you do?

Our culture encourages us to 'get'. We want more, need more, strive for more,
yet the true longing of the human soul is to give of ourselves.

"Too often we underestimate the power of a touch, a smile, a kind word, a listening ear, an honest
compliment, or the smallest act of caring, all of which have the potential to turn a life around."
–Leo F. Buscaglia

"Take what's in your hand and share it."
– Mr. Medina

You may never know the impact that your offering will make for
someone else, but you will feel the impact in your own heart.
So what's in your hand? Your lunch; your spare jacket; your time; your spare room; your
money; your words; your caring; your help? Reach out with an open hand and share.

"The value of a man resides in what he gives and not in what he is capable of receiving."
– Albert Einstein

"It is in giving that we receive"
– St Francis of Assisi

Therein lies true wealth!

Making It Personal 5

As you step into the invitation to a new page or a fresh chapter in your own story, choose to offer what's in your hand with a cheerful heart. Be ever mindful and thankful for what you have received yourself. Decide in your heart what you will give and then give it happily! No grudging giving. No coerced giving. No obligated giving. That kind of giving shrivels up the love and ends up stealing from you instead.

Give cheerfully! You just may inspire someone to step into their own story of giving.

"You don't change people's mind by the words you speak,
but you inspire change in their hearts by the life you live."
– Unknown

Leave the door of invitation always open. You may be surprised at who accepts your invitation and enters into their own adventures in sharing.

"Each man should give what he has decided in his heart to give,
not reluctantly or under compulsion,
for God loves a cheerful giver."
– 2 Corinthians 9:7

Therein lies true influence!

Making It Personal 6

Leaving a legacy is often a long way from our daily thoughts. The mark we leave as we go about our lives is often not something we are being intentional about. Yet we all do leave a legacy. We leave footprints as we walk and the path we go down will influence those who come behind us.

As you choose to...
- Open your eyes to see the needs
- Say "yes" to stepping up to the plate
- Give what's is in your hand
- Invite others to join you

...surprising adventures will be created as your story grows. Others will follow your footprints and step up to their own stories. A legacy will be created.

"Your story is the greatest legacy that you will leave to your friends.
It's the longest-lasting legacy you will leave to your heirs."
– Steve Saint

We long for more, even in spite of all we have because God has put eternity within our hearts and we long for what is truly lasting. As we participate with God in reaching out to others we, in turn, reach out and touch our own true purpose.

Therein lies true fulfillment!

Making It Personal 7

Dear God,

Today I ask that You would help me to look with eyes that see and to listen with ears that hear. May I truly notice those You place along my pathway. May I hear their stories and listen carefully for Your quiet whisper in my soul.

Help me to enjoy true purpose by having an open hand to share generously whether it is in giving my time, my care, my resources or my interest.

Thank you for Your great love and faithfulness. Help me to grow to know You better. Give me the strength and the wisdom to look and listen and act today. I pray this in Jesus' name, amen.

> "May the God of hope fill you with all joy and peace,
> as you trust in Him,
> so that you may overflow with hope
> by the power of the Holy Spirit."
> – Romans 15:13

Therein lies true hope!

Endnotes

#1 Global Issues, The Human Development
Report
www.statisticbrain.com/world-poverty-statistics/
Research date: 7/23/2012

#2 Central Intelligence Agency {US}
https://www. CIA.gov/library/publications/
the-world-factbook/geos/dr.html

#3 The Samaritan Foundation
http://www.thesamaritanfoundationdr.com

#4 Elio's book, 'Divine Passion to Help Others'
http://www.youtube.com/
watch?v=jKWHHYw9fEU

#5 Kids Alive International
http://www.kidsalive.org/around-the-world/
latin-america/dominican-republic/

#6 Mercy Ships
www.mercyships.ca

#7 New Missions
www.newmissions.org

#8 Various groups:

*Don Juan Paliza, Honorary Consul of Spain
(purchased 21 acres in Montellano)

*Mercy Ships; Steve Coetzee with Life Outreach
International (built several wells and provided
funds for 80 homes)
 http://www.lifetoday.org

*The Dorcas Sisters of the Italian Pentecostal
churches of Norhtern Europe set up a medical
clinic in Sosua.

*Dr. Park, a South Koren American surgeon funded the school in Villa Ascension.

*Kids Alive sponsored and operates the school. (see #5)

*Dream Project sponsored and operates the kindergarten and library in Ascension
http://dominicandream.org

*Mercy Ships, Mission Direct
http://www.missiondirect.org/?s=dominican+republic

*Judy Warrrington groups from Ontario, Canada and Rotary groups from Canada all combined efforts which resulted in a church, a mission service centre and a residence for volunteers.

#9 Dominican Crossroads
http://dominicancrossroads.com

#10 Servants Heart Ministries
www.servantsheartdr.org

#11 Dominican Advance
http://www.dominicanadvance.org

#12 Compassion Canada
https://www.compassion.ca

#13 Village Bridge
 http://thevillagebridge.wordpress.com/dominican-republic-bridge/project-update/

#14 Spruceland Millworks
http://www.spruceland.ca/givingBack.php

#15 International Needs Network
http://www.internationalneeds.ca/about-us

#16 Recycle HOPE (Helping Other People Eat)
http://recycle-hope.org/dr_info.php

#17 Willing Servant Ministries
http://www.willingservantministries.org/news/About%20the%20DR.html

#18 Island Light Ministries
http://www.islandlightministries.org

#19 Various groups:

Rogue Valley Fellowship of Oregon and 360 Church of Petaluma, Ca and Village Bridge (13)

#20 Nest of Love
http://www.nestoflovefoundation.org

#21 Gleaners Ontario
http://www.ontariogleaners.org

#22 Christian Life Relief International
http://www.clti.net

#23 Innova Homes in Alberta
http://www.innovahomes.ca

#24 Making it Personal /Gail Rodgers
www.gailrodgers.ca

#25 Life Outreach International
www.lifetoday.org